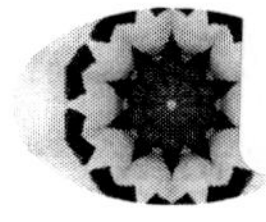

Common Passion, Different Voices

Reflections on Citizenship and Intersubjectivity

Eva Skærbæk (coordinator)
Dasa Duhaček
Elena Pulcini
Melita Richter

Series title: Travelling Concepts in Feminist Pedagogy: European Perspectives
Series editors: Clare Hemmings and Ann Kaloski-Naylor

Common Passion, Different Voices

SERIES TITLE: Travelling Concepts in Feminist Pedagogy: European Perspectives
SERIES EDITORS: Clare Hemmings and Ann Kaloski-Naylor
BOOKLET TITLE: Common Passion, Different Voices: Reflections on Citizenship and Intersubjectivity
AUTHORS: Eva Skærbæk (coordinator), Dasa Duhaček, Elena Pulcini, Melita Richter
DESIGN: Hilary Kay Doran; mandela images adapted by Josephine Wilson from Ulla Holm's photographs
PRINTING: York Publishing Services Limited, UK. www.yps-publishing.co.uk
PROOFING: Karen Coulter, Lee Ronald and Liz Sourbut
FINANCIAL SUPPORT: Centre for Women's Studies, University of York, UK www.york.ac.uk/inst/cws
and Athena 2 Advanced Thematic Network in European Women's Studies www.athena2.org
WEB: www.travellingconcepts.net
EMAIL: info@travellingconcepts.net

ISBN: 0-9553586-2-0; 978-0-9553586-2-3

First published in 2006 by
Raw Nerve Books Limited
Centre for Women's Studies, University of York, York YO10 5DD, England
www.rawnervebooks.co.uk

British Library Cataloguing-in publication Data.
A catalogue record for this book is available from the British Library.

Series Preface

Travelling Concepts in Feminist Pedagogy: European Perspectives *is one of the projects currently taking place under the umbrella of Athena, which is a Socrates Thematic Network Project bringing together over 100 Women's and Gender Studies programmes, institutes and documentation centres across Europe: www.athena2.org*

The twenty-four partners working within *Travelling Concepts* have come together in the shared desire to track the movement of key feminist ideas across the geographical, political and cultural complexity that is contemporary Europe.

The partners in *Travelling Concepts* come from fourteen different European countries, and are housed within a range of disciplines or interdisciplinary contexts. Some of us work within Gender or Women's Studies departments, centres or institutes, while others negotiate the specific challenges of feminist research and pedagogy from within 'home' disciplines. Some of us work centrally within academic inquiry, while others straddle academic and activist interests, or teach within a broader educational field, such as adult education. These differing contexts invariably produce different intellectual and political agendas within the group, yet there are a number of points of commonality that we have been able to identify, and the differences have also been productive arenas of inquiry in their own right.

Intellectually and politically, thinking about travelling concepts in feminist pedagogy means foregrounding questions of exclusion, power and silence, among us and in Europe more generally. This work has to attend not only to racism and heterosexism as well as sexism, but also to the specificities of whose movements are constrained and curtailed, whose left more open. Within the work of *Travelling Concepts* West/East barriers proved difficult to overcome, as did presumptions based on generational differences, and silences around whiteness. We have been concerned to make sure that the work we produce reflects directly on these issues and is an invested, politically and intellectually charged map of conceptual travel, one in which we are all staked and located.

One of the ways we hope to develop broader dialogue is through this book series. Each of the four publications addresses a cluster of key concepts and each has been written by a different group of feminist academics from different European countries and disciplinary backgrounds. We look forward to further discussion and invite you to our participatory web site: www.travellingconcepts.net

Books

ReSisters in Conversation: Representation Responsibility Complexity Pedagogy
Giovanna Covi (coordinator), Joan Anim-Addo, Liana Borghi, Luz Gómez García, Sara Goodman, Sabine Grenz, Mina Karavanta.
ISBN: 0-9553586-0-4; 978-0-9553586-0-9

Practising Interdisciplinarity in Gender Studies
Veronica Vasterling (coordinator), Enikő Demény, Clare Hemmings, Ulla Holm, Päivi Korvajärvi, Theodossia-Soula Pavlidou,
ISBN: 0-9553586-1-2; 978-0-9553586-1-6

Common Passion, Different Voices: Reflections on Citizenship and Intersubjectivity
Eva Skærbæk (coordinator), Dasa Duhaček, Elena Pulcini, Melita Richter.
ISBN: 0-9553586-2-0; 978-0-9553586-2-3

Teaching Subjects In Between: Feminist Politics, Disciplines, Generations
Therese Garstenauer (coordinator), Josefina Bueno Alonso, Silvia Caporale Bizzini, Biljana Kašić, Iris van der Tuin.
ISBN: 0-9553586-3-9; 978-0-9553586-3-0

Details of all four books are available on www.rawnervebooks.co.uk
Books can be ordered direct from Raw Nerve or from good bookshops.

Contents

Acknowledgements

First and foremost the authors want to express gratitude for the loving and precious help from Clare Hemmings, the leader of the *Travelling Concepts* group. Her empowering stamina has helped us more than words can express through all the process of elaborating this work and particularly in overcoming difficult periods along the way.

We also want to thank editor Ann Kaloski from Raw Nerve Books for her friendly but firm way of supporting us towards publication.

To Jan Malabotta we owe thanks for the graphical presentation of different phases of our conceptual maps.

Introduction

Eva Skærbæk

This booklet proudly presents the collaborative work of four scholars from different disciplinary backgrounds and orientations: Dasa Duhaček from former Yugoslavia/Serbia, Elena Pulcini from Italy, Melita Richter from former Yugoslavia/Croatia/Italy and Eva Skærbæk from Denmark/Norway. Proudly, because this publication reveals to the reader as it did to the members of this group how much there is to gain from working across and in-between differences in disciplines, age and personalities.

As part of a larger project concerned with 'Travelling Concepts in Feminist Pedagogy: European Perspectives', our group originally chose to subject *intersubjectivity* and *citizenship* to sustained analysis. Citizenship represents the practical, the political; intersubjectivity represents the basis, the theory. This choice of concepts tells a story about our common ground in feminist thought and its critique of the modern Cartesian and liberal subject *and* a common engagement in today's society. Both concepts are focused through gender/sex difference, which is the oldest known difference inscribed in language and has been experienced right up to modern times as a basic condition of life. Each concept forms an ideal circle, which partly overlap each other, leaving a joint space for the positioning of other concepts.

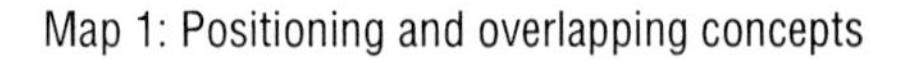

Map 1: Positioning and overlapping concepts

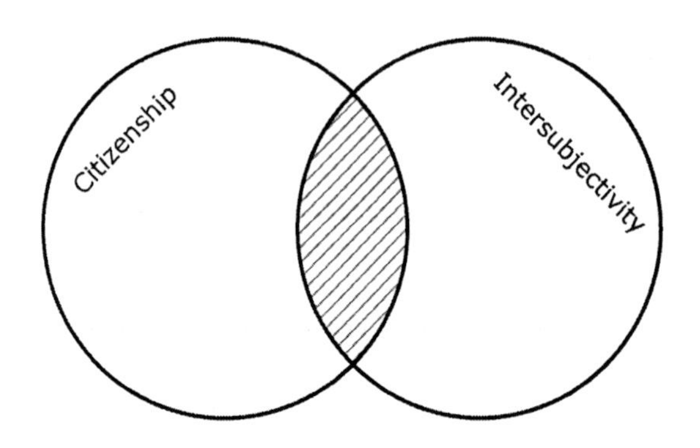

Initially we came up with the following two questions as general guidelines for our discussion:

- What is the impact of these concepts in different cultural, geopolitical and professional contexts and daily life practices?

- What do we mean when we conceptualise these notions in our research and teaching?

'You have a plan until you get another.' This is our experience too. Entering late in the process, Elena triggered one of the significant difficulties in the process of collaborating. Within our group, for various reasons, members did not or could not give priority to the group meetings, resulting in a rather fragmented and at times frustrating debate. When, in addition, Elena chose concepts other than the agreed ones, she became the 'disturbance' usually associated with 'gender', i.e. women, because she has also consistently refused to ground these concepts in her daily life practice. This 'disturbance', however, fuelled the discussion and maybe also the process of working as a group. Suddenly deadlines were no longer a problem, but more a challenge. Manuscripts kept coming in at all hours, indicating different life and working styles, but most of all bearing witness to a strong engagement with the ongoing debates, which were becoming intrinsically interrelated. And we found ourselves not only enjoying working together, but also becoming more and more aware of the importance of Athena 2, the larger group process we are all a part of, for allowing us this dialogue transgressing disciplines, cultures, personalities and work arenas.

We couldn't all attend all meetings, and therefore we had to give up on the initial objective of discussing our papers in person. This influenced the structure of this booklet. Inspired by *Feminist Contentions, A Philosophical Exchange*, 1995, and some of the editions of the journal *Signs*, this booklet consists of four initial papers, and our comments on them, followed by interactions and responses between the authors. Although this was something of an emergency model, it suddenly took on a life of its own and began moving and flowing like a piece of music. Starting with three instruments following the notes (citizenship and intersubjectivity), and one using counterpoint (globalisation and reciprocity), the tempo changed from *adagio* to *allegretto*, and ended in *crescendo*, and the sentiment went from *con amore* to *con brio*.

The metaphor of music is not accidental. Music is global, and yet it has its local characteristics and concrete daily life practices. Answering a question from the audience concerning changes in a certain piece of music when directed in another country with another orchestra, an Australian conductor spoke of how different the same piece of music became and how wonderful she thought that was. In other words, although both the written notes and the conductor are the same, the music becomes influenced by musicians, culture and history; different but still recognisable. In the same way, concepts change due to varying interpretations of their meanings, to different personal, local and disciplinary positions. The reason for choosing citizenship and intersubjectivity as key concepts was to strike a theme that would allow us to engage in a discussion that could challenge if not transcend these differences. And so it did.

Map 2: Integrating other concepts, their interdependence and rise in complexity

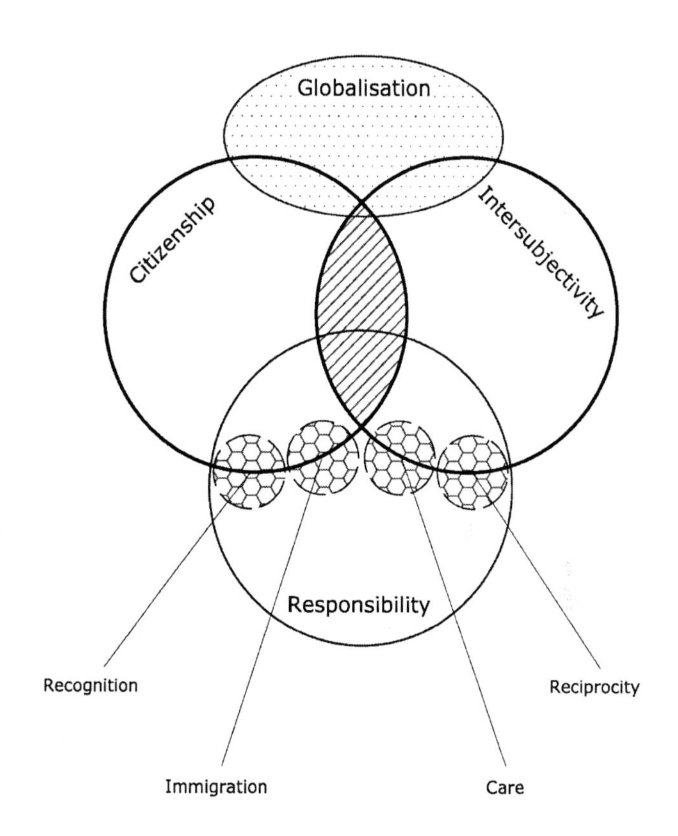

In observing citizenship critically we all agree that there is a need to take into account its twofold nature: 1. the normative – indicating

a wide range of rights and 2. the practice – the lived experience. In the relationship between rights and practice, citizenship should be understood as a dynamic process and not as a straightforward outcome. In this frame, Elena and Melita have a passionate debate about citizenship in a globalised world, in which the more ideal perspective of philosophy and the more down to earth socio-political point of view clash. In order to deal with responsibility and care, Elena suggests a more complex definition of globalisation than the one that continues to see the world in opposing terms: *us*, the rich Western world and *them*, the poor world. From this perspective, it is possible to transcend all ethical, national and religious differences by seeing *us* as members of the same 'human genre'. Dasa and Melita are both marked by their experiences of the war and what followed: the changes and challenges of their multi-ethnic and multicultural society, especially in relation to women. Dasa's main theme is the relationship of another key concept to the status of citizenship – that of responsibility. Could responsibility to/for the Other allow ethics to permeate politics? Melita suggests introducing the idea of mobile citizenship in order to recognise immigrants and other excluded human beings as participative social actors. And Eva is concerned with how to overcome the chasm between women's strong participation in the local politics of everyday life and their lack of inclusion in European and global politics and, last but not least, how to transform frustration into ways of acting.

Focusing on intersubjectivity gave rise to a debate about the relevance of the concept. Arguing that intersubjectivity in the Habermasian definition overlooks the concrete dimension lived by its subjects,

Elena suggests replacing it with the concept of reciprocity. Dasa and Eva, inspired by Beauvoir, maintain that intersubjectivity, in its emphasis on the concrete situated Other, has the potential to connect ethics and politics. And thus care ended up being a key concept for all of us, although in different ways. Melita comments on Eva's definition of care as an *existential condition of life*, transcending the gendered division of working spheres and embracing the universal, and wonders if this is in fact politics. To Elena's focus on care for the self as necessary for care for the other, Dasa responds that while the care of the self is recognised and deployed, care for the other has rarely been implemented despite all declarations to the contrary. When care for the self is a primary concern, it ramifies into a political priority, and thus becomes inconsistent with care for the other. Care for the self consequently does not entail a view of citizenship as a responsibility for the other. In spite of conceptual overlaps regarding care, this discussion points to a major discrepancy amongst ourselves about ethics, and therefore also about politics.

This structure and method of approaching and comprehending the key concepts, and the questions mentioned above, show how challenging it is to work across different professional and life experiences. Whether this is due to personality, discipline, culture, experience, or maybe due to the fact that we all belong to a generation raised to be Cartesian subjects, is as impossible as it is unproductive to address.

Although we all find it a useful, if not necessary, presupposition in order to understand ourselves and each other's thoughts, our discussion demonstrates how reluctant we are, and how difficult we find it, to connect abstract academic thinking with daily life practices. Since there is much less reference to personal experiences and daily life practices in our booklet than we wished, we hope that the reader will be able to read between the lines. And finally, we should add that we have deliberately allowed our 'product' to be open-ended. Rather than close our (reflecting) dialogue we want to invite and provoke further reflections on the issues we have been discussing.

One of Karen Blixen's mottos was '*Je responderay*', I will respond (1979). The common ground of every text and author here is a desire to respond not only to the challenges of daily life and professional work experienced by women, but also to bridge the North-South and East-West divide, both conceptually and experientially.

Bibliography

Blixen, Karen (1979) 'On mottoes of my life' *Daguerreotypes and Other Essays* Chicago: The University of Chicago Press.

Position Papers

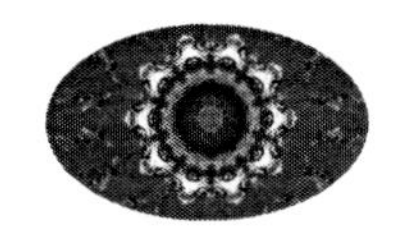

Ethics and/in Politics: Towards Citizenship as Responsibility to the Other

Dasa Duhaček

What kind of relationship between (political) community and its individual members should we privilege? Or, to put it succinctly: what model of citizenship should we privilege?

This of course opens up the issue of the political; moreover, the political with a view to the ethical. Some concepts, such as obligation, consent and duty, can be traced to mainstream liberal tradition as attributes of citizenship, whether accepted or contested. For me, the main question concerns the relationship of another concept to the status of citizenship – that of responsibility; or, more specifically, I would like to explore citizenship as responsibility to (and perhaps even for) the Other.

Locke claimed that the decisive step in establishing the contractual relation of citizenship is consent (of any man – sic!), be it express or tacit. In order to specify the conditions of this relationship, or rather, to state which privileges the status of citizenship will be grounded on, expounding on tacit consent, he goes on to say: 'that every Man, that hath any Possession, or Enjoyment, of any part of the Dominions of any Government, doth thereby give his tacit Consent, and is as far forth obliged to Obedience to the Laws of that Government, during such Enjoyment, as any one under it; (…); and in Effect, it reaches as far as the very being of anyone within the Territories of that Government' (Locke, [1698] 1992: 347-8). What Locke begins to unfold here is a relationship between citizens and their respective governments in a format that has been more or less present in any subsequent treatise on this subject, i.e. recognising only the responsibility of citizens to their government and *vice versa*, the responsibility of the government to its citizens. To date '*consent* legitimates government' and the 'ballot box' is 'the mechanism whereby the individual citizen expresses political preferences and citizens as whole periodically confer authority on government to enact laws and regulate economic and social life' (Held, 1997: 86). This rightly gives citizenship a privileged status that designates it as belonging to a political community, inasmuch as it entails a right/privilege (to presumably receive protection) and a duty (to follow regulations of a thus contractually formed government). Both of these relationships necessitate and allow for extensive elaborations, however in this text I am interested in discussing yet another relation: namely the responsibility *for the government* that citizens give either their 'express' or their 'tacit' consent to. Although there is no explicit mention of it, there is no other conclusion to be drawn: citizens are the ones who should bear that responsibility.

This relationship of personal/individual responsibility *for* the government we choose translates into *our* political responsibility for *our political choices*; or, responsibility of all those who belong to a (political) community. The complexity of the problem is that this relationship of personal responsibility spreads, or to put it more precisely, bifurcates: firstly, to other members of one's own, my own, community and secondly, to members of other political communities. The latter form of responsibility is shared with other members of my own community and structures collective responsibility which is always already political (Arendt, 2003). It is responsibility for what my government has done in my name.

This theoretical analysis has a personal meaning for me. The country I lived in was broken up in a series of devastating wars; thousands were killed, wounded and raped, millions were displaced. Simone de Beauvoir reminds us that floods, earthquakes or pestilence are, metaphorically speaking, 'the scourge of god' and that, consequently, we suffer differently from the effects of earthquakes than from the consequences of wars, the wars being of our own making (Beauvoir, 1972). Hence, for me, the importance of the issue of responsibility. In resolving it I found it useful to draw some analogies between the events in Germany from 1933-1945 and the events that took place in the Balkans in the 1990s. My assumption was that for the citizens of Serbia there is a lesson to be learnt from the history of German Nazism. In searching for some answers I turned to Hannah Arendt, since she based her political theory on her own experiences of those times. I attempted to establish whether Arendt's theory could be used as a point of departure for an analysis of what has happened in the Balkans. Furthermore, and on a personal note, Arendt's work allowed me first and foremost to mourn: it allowed me to be angry; to get over it, and to move on; to forsake and renounce certain times once and for all, and yet remain within those times. Her writing made me see that it was possible to stay in a place and to finally leave it – at the same time, to critically look upon and recognise my whole world for what it was – as it was falling apart. I am not sure I would have had the same experience had I had the opportunity to hear her in person and I am not sure I would have even liked her, but I am sure her words would have spoken to me – as they do now.

However, although they raise the issue of responsibility for the past, the analogies between post-war Serbia and post-war Germany for the most part do not hold regarding the future, as Serbia is now going through a difficult multilayered transitional process, the goal of which I see as rebuilding its citizenship. As a political theorist with a background in philosophy, who is at the same time a teacher, I think that the question, used as a point of departure for this text – i.e. which model of citizenship should we privilege? – is a critical one. Futhermore, the keyword in the search for answers, which will be grounded in facing the past and looking towards the future, should be responsibility, meaning responsibility to/for the Other.

I find the most emphatic statement about *my* responsibility for the *Other* to be found in the writings of Emmanuel Lévinas: 'I speak of responsibility as the essential, primary and fundamental structure of subjectivity (…) I understand responsibility as responsibility for the Other …' (Lévinas, 1985: 95). The force and the credibility of this enunciation comes from the claim that it is the *face* (of the Other) that speaks and demands this response/ibility.[1] This raises Lévinas' theory above abstract universalism and consequently makes it more easily translatable into *praxis*; then perhaps ethics can permeate politics. And what places an additional burden on me, and what makes it even more demanding, is that this is *not* a symmetrical relation inasmuch as there must *not* be a comfortable expectation of reciprocity; because the response which would take myself as the Other into account (in the eyes of my Other) would be entirely his/her affair.

In order to make this project feasible it has to be defined and therefore circumscribed, much as, for example, Adrienne Rich has clearly delineated the space of her own accountability to the (nation) state of which she is a citizen in 'Notes Towards Politics of Location' (Rich, 1986).

I single out Adrienne Rich as one of my personal favorites, since she has spoken from the first person singular when claiming accountability, and has pointed to the many complexities of the matter, especially when we start translating these claims into (political) statements that aim for change. Among some of the complexities that she perceptively mentions is the difficulty of saying 'I' and, following that, taking a leap towards saying 'we'. The assumption is that this 'we' constitutes political collectivity and is therefore a premise for political action.

I also see that the unfolding of feminist theories within the flow of its wide stream – differences within the current notwithstanding – all move in a general direction towards raising awareness of the Other, sensitising to the needs of the Other, resisting exclusionary practices, of black, queer, third world, postcolonial, or just poor, old, sick, hurt, wounded. All this with a view to, as Donna Haraway would put it, 'disarming the state' – her Livermore Action Group included witches, engineers, elders, perverts, Christians, mothers, and Leninists (Haraway, 1990).

Quite differently, Sartre claimed that 'we' as a common denominator of 'I' and 'you' most easily comes into existence in the face of a third as the common enemy! This perspective comes from mainstream philosophy where the position of the Other in its modern variance is best exemplified in Hegel's Master-Slave narrative. As we know, the recognition of the Other/by the Other is always already a battle where life is at stake. Establishing an I-we relation in matters of political engagement may be further complicated, as when for example Judith Butler asks of Lévinas: 'What if there is an Other who does violence to another Other?' (Butler, 2004: 138). Even this formulation points to the fact that the I-we problem is fundamentally the problem of the Other.

The issue raised here is: While assessing the concept of the political today, is there a turn to ethics? (Garber, 2000), and, if so, what are the consequences for politics? Can we even conceive of a politics that does not necessitate a 'turn to ethics' because it is always already turned to ethics? We would, however, need an ethics that would not at the same time call for a Nietzschean critique of morality, because it would have disassociated itself from any 'Christian morality' and would have embarked on a civic, secular and consequently a politically mature citizenship. Arendt claims that the political act in its unique performative character is comparable to art. Of course, the political she has in mind is far removed from the *real politik* that we encounter daily and is recognised if and only if it brings freedom to bear on (any segment of) our world. But she also realises that discovering freedom as the 'lost treasure of revolutions' is as rare as 'unicorns and fairy queens' (Arendt, 1993: 5).

Many have addressed the complex issue of bringing ethics into the political. Thus Tzvetan Todorov, in his thought-provoking study entitled *We and Others* (Todorov, 1989), has researched how thinkers relevant to our contemporary world deal with the issue of the Other (although his research is limited to French modern thought, it has analysed models of exclusionary thinking well). This study brings to light many significant points that treat the (problem of the) Other. However, Todorov, as with many of his contemporaries, sustains a theoretically sharp divide, a chasm, between ethics and politics, or to be specific he carries this gap over from *real politik* without even remotely suggesting the possibility of bridging or overcoming it. Here I disagree with Todorov because I think that unless that possibility is theoretically articulated it is unlikely to come about (which is certainly not to say that a theoretical outline alone is enough to create its reality). But more importantly, it is interesting to note that not only is there no mention of Beauvoir's ground-breaking thesis that *Woman is the (model of) the Other* (Beauvoir, 1949), but his text has no gender perspective whatsoever.

One way to connect the political practice of citizenship with care for the Other is through the concept of intersubjectivity, where intersubjectivity is understood as the theoretical underpinning of this political practice. Perhaps then intersubjectivity can create a bridge between ethics and politics. However, this would require an unfolding of the concept of intersubjectivity, since there is more than one way of understanding it. For example, it is woven into Habermas' theory, as a 'reciprocal recognition' that exists 'in conjunction with the correlative independence of the other' (1993: 43). Although the terminology and the wording is in its place (intersubjectivity, reciprocity, even the 'other'), the Habermasian approach concerns a *generalised other* more than it allows for *the care of the concrete other*; this approach has therefore rightly been the subject of extensive critique from and within feminist theory, most notably in the work of Nancy Fraser (1997). In her criticism she not only names the general problems of normative ideals and the liberal model of the public sphere, but also points to concrete ways of moving forward from lamenting exclusionary practices, towards tipping the scales in favour of measures of inclusion (of the other/s); she concludes that we need to think of a multiplicity of publics. In this respect, Fraser promotes in particular the political significance of civil society. The critical role of civil society was, in the case of Serbia, carried out mostly by women and women's groups; this was the case in respect to peace, antimilitarist and antinationalist activism, as well as in building opposition to the Milosevic regime (e.g. in the fields of education, cultural production, media, etc.)[2].

Intersubjectivity on the other hand, can also inspiringly be drawn from Beauvoir's *Ethics of Ambiguity*. Given the pivotal contribution of defining woman as the Other, marked as such not only by mainstream philosophy but also by the whole of civilisation, Beauvoir's analysis is very nuanced; for example, she asks how the mechanism of taking on responsibility may work, since she is adamant that responsibility is not – and neither should it be – equally distributed. She claims that responsibility lies first and foremost with those who hold power; namely responsibility should be allocated in proportion to one's position in the structures of decision-making. Following this through, two choices are: to negate the connection between power and responsibility or, affirming this connection, to redefine citizenship as a 'burden of responsibility' and thereby empower those who have hitherto been stripped of power.

Importantly, this issue, raised within a contemporary world, always greatly benefits from a context-specific (geopolitical, cultural) placement. Within the context of the Western Balkans it is mostly women, some of whom are organised in feminist and peace activist groups, that are at least exemplifying by their political activity how the Others within their respective political communities may be faced, be they lesbian, Roma, belonging to (an) other ethnicity, nation, religion or any Other; this is an implicit restructuring and reconceptualising of citizenship as a responsibility to the Other.

Notes

[1]. In his philosophy Lévinas assigns to the category of *face* a central place for a representation of the Other in its concrete individualized and material form, thereby putting on (every) me the weight of responsibility for the Other.

[2] There are also representatives of feminist theory that find Habermasian discursive ethics acceptable. For example, Jodi Dean (1996) claims that it is open ended and contextual.

Bibliography

Arendt, Hannah (2003) 'Collective Responsibility' in *Responsibility and Judgment,* Schocken Books, New York.

______ (1993) 'Preface' to *Between Past and Future,* Penguin Books, New York.

______ (1958) *The Human Condition*, University of Chicago Press, Chicago and New York.

Beauvoir, Simone de (1949) *Le Deuxiemme Sexe*, Gallimard, Paris.

______ (1972) *Pour une Morale de l'ambguitè*, Gallimard, Paris.

Bernstein, Richard (2000) *Odgovornost filozofa (Responsibility of a Philosopher),* Beogradski krug, Beograd.

Butler, Judith (2004) *Precarious Life, The Powers of Mounrning and Violence*, Verso, London and New York.

Dean, Jodi (1996) *Solidarity of Strangers*, University of California Press, Berkley and Los Angeles.

Fraser, Nancy (1997) 'Rethinking the Public Sphere' in *Justice Interruptus*, Routledge, New York and London.

Garber, Marjorie et al, eds (2000) *The Turn to Ethics,* Routledge, New York.

Habermas, Jurgen (1993) *Justification and Application*, MIT, Cambridge, Mass. and London.

Haraway, Donna (1990) 'A Manifesto for Cyborgs: Science, Technology and Socialist Feminism in the 1980s' in Linda Nicholson, ed, *Feminism and Postmodernism*, Routledge, New York.

Held, David (1998) 'Democracy: From City-States to a Cosmopolitan Order?' in Robert Goodin and Philip and Petit, eds *Contemporary Political Philosophy*, Blackwell Publishers, Oxford.

Lévinas, Emmanuel (1985) *Ethics and Infinity*, Duquesne University Press, Pittsburgh.

Locke, John (1992) *An Essay Concerning the True Original, Extent, and End of Civil Government*, Cambridge University Press, Cambridge.

Rich, Adrienne (1986) 'Notes Towards a Politics of Location', in *Blood, Bread and Poetry: Selected Prose 1979-1985*, London, Virago.

Todorov, Tzvetan (1989) *Nous et les Autres*, Editions du Seuil, Paris.

Responsibility and Care in the Global Age

Elena Pulcini

1

I would like to begin by saying that my emphasis on the concept of the 'Global Age' (Albrow, 1996) is due to the fact that in my opinion the process of globalisation produces some radical changes to modernity that make us reflect upon new challenges, the first being that some concepts need to be rethought (especially the concept of responsibility, but also intersubjectivity and citizenship, which we are dealing with here) in the light of these changes (Bauman, 1998; Robertson, 1992; Geertz, 1999). So, before dealing with this problem, I think it is necessary to clarify some issues concerning globalisation.

First of all, I would like to stress that globalisation is not just an economic process that creates worldwide inequalities, requiring the problem of the distribution of resources to be rethought in line with principles of equity, or the problem of citizenship to be reconsidered from a global viewpoint (Habermas,1998). We risk taking too narrow a view if we choose to deal with the problem merely in terms of justice, rights and citizenship. This would mean continuing to see the world in oppositional terms: 'us' (the rich, Western world), and 'them' (the poor world, the 'fourth world').

Obviously I do not wish to deny the enormous and very real

problem of planetary inequalities, but what I would like to claim is that the radically new nature of globalisation is that it creates a *single world* in which there are potentially no barriers between *us* and *them* any more. It is a total process that impacts on economics and politics, subjectivity and the imagination, communication and culture, the environment and nature (Beck, 1999; Bauman, 1999).

And this means that no-one is immune from the effects that it causes. Globalisation is planetary interdependence and the end of immunity (as suggested by 9/11). The West, the main agent in globalisation, is also the *spectator* and *victim*: a somewhat powerless spectator and potential victim of 'global risks' (Beck, 1997,1986; Giddens 1990) such as the nuclear threat, global warming, viral epidemics, environmental disasters and terrorism.

Globalisation is the loss of borders, it is the creation of a world that seems at the same time infinitely *open* due to the disappearance and weakening of borders, and closed, as we are now lacking a clearly distinct and identifiable 'elsewhere' whose resources can be exploited without end and upon whom we can offload the undesirable effects of our own 'unsustainable' development. There is no longer an 'elsewhere' into which Western civilisation – as has always happened since the beginning of modernity – can expand and prosper.

And – potentially – there is no longer the 'other'. The other lives in our neighbourhood, mixes into the chaos of our metropolises, passes beyond confines, across territories, in frenzied and ungovernable migration. This other is the potential victim, like us, of the dangers that go before every difference and also before every inequality.

In my view, this very uncomfortable scenario gives rise to new possibilities and perspectives: the global age contains the *chance* to bring the planet's individuals together under a common destiny, to create new *forms of alliance and solidarity* based on the awareness that we all, beyond all ethnic, national, religious *differences*, are members of the same 'human genre', affected by the same events (Pulcini, 2001a).

2

But it is only an *objective chance*, that requires subjects who are capable of making the most of this possibility, of giving fitting responses to the new challenges of the global era. Taking this chance means taking *responsibility* for the global processes that seem to escape all control (Bauman, 1999). And this is all the more important as, at least since the beginning of modernity, *politics*, entrusted with controlling and decision-making functions, also seems to be overrun by a crisis that questions roles and perspectives. Thus, before we ask *politics*, thwarted by the crisis in its governing and decision-making capacity (the crisis of State sovereignty), we need to ask *individuals* themselves to take on this responsibility.

The first thing that comes to mind is the invitation that Hans Jonas made some decades ago (Jonas, 1979). The emerging nuclear threat – he claimed – creates for the first time the possibility of losing the world that hosts us and the life of humanity. This radicalization of evil generates new fears and therefore new possibilities to relate with the other and with the world, to become responsible for them.

To take up such an invitation requires an awareness that global risks are not something inevitable and ungovernable: unlike natural 'dangers', global risks are the result of human creation, of the Promethean *hubris* of the *homo faber* (Anders, 1956; Arendt, 1958). Human action, the technical action of man – guided by the *acquisitive drive* (Pulcini, 2001) – has endangered the very life of humanity. For the first time, the world can no longer be taken for granted, it is no longer a fact, but is becoming something that *needs caring for* so it can continue to exist.

Therefore, responsibility must not be seen as something that has to be, as a deontological imperative that we impose upon ourselves due to an abstract moral law. First of all it is *care* (for life, the world, the other): a care that is *emotionally* triggered by the *fear of loss*, by the awareness that without care the world and life itself are exposed to destruction and death; or if nothing else, to a degraded life that is not worth living.

It is not a matter of saying 'we must be responsible', but of responding to the plea, to the 'call' – as Emmanuel Lévinas would put it (Lévinas, 1961) – that is imperiously made to us from that which hosts us and makes *our own life* possible.

3

Therefore, the concept of care we are dealing with is only in part the parental and maternal paradigm as proposed by Jonas and more recently by Carol Gilligan (1982). A mother's care for her child in fact originates from love for the other (the child) due to its weakness and vulnerability; it assumes there is a hierarchical dissonance between the

Self and the Other. Instead, care for the Other is inextricably bound to care for the Self, it is the recognition of our own vulnerability, dependence and finiteness.

In part, this takes us back to the idea of 'birth', dealt with in female thought by Hannah Arendt (1958), and in part to the idea of 'neediness' as proposed by Martha Nussbaum (Nussbaum, 2001). Indeed, for Arendt, birth is the representation *par excellence* of the fragility of the human condition, looked upon positively as a virtue. Fragility, or if we prefer, lack of self-sufficiency, becomes a virtue when we recognise the importance of the 'world', of the plurality that links together every single human being, putting us all on the same level. If birth is the event that brings us into this world, from our very origins handing us over to the plurality of the world and relations with the other, then we must recognise fragility as a dimension that constitutes mankind [sic!].

We can also say that the event of birth is a sign that recalls the origin, the very fact that we *had an origin*; that is, it recalls that we are filial, animal and therefore dependent and vulnerable and ontologically exposed to otherness. Being aware of our fragility therefore transforms us into subjects mindful of our limits and dependence, into 'needy' subjects, we could say, developing the concept of 'neediness' proposed by Nussbaum; and thus we are always open to *contamination* by the 'other than the Self' that forms our intimate make-up.

This vision of the subject – which I cannot go into here, but have proposed elsewhere in my criticism of the paradigm of the modern Cartesian subject and my normative proposal of the notion of the *contaminated subject* (Pulcini, 2006) – is what allows me to separate the concept of care from its 'maternalistic' and altruistic implications (Pulcini, 2003). Instead, I would like to propose a meaning of *care* that is intimately triggered by my notion of the *contaminated subject*: assumed, as a subject that is not closed in its pretension of self-sufficiency, but open, exposed to the Other, because it is passed through by a lack, or a constitutional 'wound' (Bataille, 1973), that makes it conscious of its insufficiency and of its inescapable need for the Other.

From this perspective, care is not to be understood as something that derives from the attitude of putting the Other first, typical of maternal psychology, but as the answer to a need for the Self: for a Self exposed to contamination.

In other words, care is the answer for a subject conscious of its own vulnerability and dependence, its own 'neediness': the subject opens up to the Other and takes care of the Other due to the awareness that it needs caring for too. We can actually say that the needy subject is capable of care only in this sense, that is, only if it recognises it is in need of care.

It is here, I could say, that the cycle of *reciprocity* begins (Mauss, 1985; Caillé, 1998; Pulcini, 2001). I prefer to speak of 'reciprocity' and not of 'intersubjectivity', in the Habermasian sense of the term (Habermas, 1981). Indeed, despite its virtue of having shown the limits of the modern (Cartesian) paradigm that defines the subject as consciousness and underlining the importance of the relational aspect, theories of intersubjectivity risk reducing subjectivity to a purely socio-linguistic construction, putting rational subjects orientated towards building a communicative sphere at the origin of the interaction by virtue of a presumed bent towards understanding and relationship.

In this respect, there is a marked lack of attention to the problem of motive at the basis of relational and communicative action in much theoretical work on intersubjectivity. This work tends to overlook the concrete, experiential dimension lived by subjects; as a consequence, it precludes the possibility of rethinking the subject itself in light of the ideas of neediness and contamination as premises for a *reciprocal caring relation* founded on the precondition of fragility and vulnerability.

In contrast, the idea of 'reciprocity' allows this aspect to be enhanced. In particular I am thinking of the way in which it has been reproposed within anti-utilitarian reflection inspired by Mauss (Caillé, 1998; Godbout, 1992), which closely links it to the *paradigm of the gift* and the concrete and symbolic dynamics that giving engenders. Here reciprocity is understood as a relational cycle in which everyone is always and simultaneously the giver and the receiver, taking action and receiving; in which the desire to give is triggered by the awareness that we ourselves have also received, the recognition that we are at the same time the subject/object of a gift. And I would like to add that this awareness is triggered by the perception of our own insufficiency, fragility, neediness and the consequent appearance of our desire for a bond, our desire to belong.

In short, the concept of 'reciprocity' implies what I have defined as an *anthropology of neediness* (Pulcini, 2001), which allows us to free the concept of *care* from precisely the twofold burden of *altruism* and *having to be*, at the same time giving it back that emotional motivation lacking in the concept of responsibility, both in its ontological and deontological senses.

This is all the more legitimate in the global age: indeed, here it appears clear that *care for the Other* (person, humanity, world) is inextricably bound to *care for the Self*, since, as humans inhabiting the same world, we all belong to the same planet, are exposed to the same risks and are called upon to respond to the same challenges, caught up as we are by a common destiny.

Bibliography

Albrow, Martin (1996) *The Global Age. State and Society beyond Modernity*, Polity Press, Cambridge.

Anders, Günther (1956) *Die Antiquiertheit der Menschen*, C.H.Beck, München.

Arendt, Hannah (1958) *The Human Condition*, University of Chicago Press, Chicago.

Bataille, Georges (1973) *Sur Nietzsche, Oeuvres Complètes*, Gallimard, Paris, vol.VI.

Bauman, Zygmut (1993) *Postmodern Ethics*, Blackwell Publishers, Oxford UK and Cambridge USA.

_____ (1998) *Globalization. The Human Consequences*, Polity Press-Blackwell Publishers, Cambridge-Oxford.

_____ (1999) *In Search of Politics*, Polity Press, Cambridge.

Beck, Ulrich (1997) *Was ist Globalisierung?*, Suhrkamp Verlag, Frankfurt am Main.

_____ (1986) *Risikogesellschaft. Auf dem Weg in eine andere Moderne*, Suhrkamp Verlag, Frankfurt am Main.

Caillé, Alain (1998) *Il terzo paradigma. Antropologia filosfica del dono*, Bollati Boringhieri, Torino.

Geertz, Clifford (1999) *Mondo globale, mondi locali,* Il Mulino, Bologna.

Giddens, Anthony (1990) *The Consequences of Modernity*, Polity Press, Cambridge.

Gilligan, Carol (1982) *In a Different Voice*, Harvard Univ. Press, Cambridge.

Godbout, Jacques T. (1992) *L'esprit du don*, La Découverte, Paris.

Habermas, Jürgen (1981) *Theorie des kommunikativen Handelns*, Suhrkamp Verlag, Frankfurt am Main.

_____ (1998) *Die Postnationale Konstellation*, Suhrkamp Verlag, Frankfurt am Main.

Jonas, Hans (1979) *Das Prinzip Verantwortung*, Insel Verlag, Frankfurt am Main.

Lévinas, Emmanuel (1961) *Totalité et infini*, Nijoff, La Haye.

Mauss, Marcel (1985) *Essai sur le don* (1923-24), in *Sociologie et anthropologie*, Presses Univ. de France, Paris.

Nancy, Jean Luc (1993) *Le sens du monde*, Galilée, Paris.

Nussbaum, Martha (2001) *Upheavals of Thought. The Intelligence of Emotions*, Cambridge Univ. Press.

Pulcini, Elena (2001) *L'individuo senza passioni. Individualismo moderno e perdita del legame sociale*, Bollati-Boringhieri, Torino.

_____ (2001a) L'Io globale: crisi del legame sociale e nuove forme di solidarietà, in Dimitri D'Andrea, Elena Pulcini (eds.), *Filosofie della globalizzazione*, ETS, Pisa.

_____ (2003) *Il potere di unire. Femminile, desiderio, cura*, Bollati Boringhieri, Torino.

_____ (2006) *The Contaminated Subject: Passions, Power and Care*, website http://www.travellingconcepts.net

Robertson, Roland (1992) *Globalization, Social Theory and Global Culture*, Sage, London.

Women Experiencing Citizenship
Melita Richter

1

I would like to start by contextualising my interest in the key concepts *intersubjectivity* and *citizenship* chosen for our analyses, and illustrate both why they play a central role in my life and how it is impossible to separate them from my own life experience.

Despite the fact that I have never had the experience of living in a country without being a citizen with full rights, I have witnessed different ways of experiencing citizenship in different states and normative systems led by different ideologies. At the same time, I have been able to observe from the distance 'of the migrant' the changes in the interpretation of citizenship in my own country, or rather my former country, which was wiped out between 1991 and 1995 by the brutality of a war generated by nationalistic folly. While the destruction of former Yugoslavia was taking place, the first to register a deep sense of loss were the women – loss of rights, and loss of their complex, expansive, plural identity.

The testimony of Vesna Teršelić allows us to enter into the general mood of the women of Yugoslavia in that period:

> I remember the summer of '91, the heat and the oppressive feeling

> of anxiety. I also remember having this need to do something, a need that I felt like a pain in my stomach. The space we worked in, we breathed in, the space we had been building for years, began to dissolve, shrink, and disappear. During that humid summer it became completely clear to me that all that we had built by way of Green Movements and Women's Groups was sinking from day to day.[1]

Further testimony, from the feminist Vesna Kesić, describes the loss of the rights of women and their new marginalisation. However, it also mentions the rebellion of women against the renewed patriarchal wave that was surging over them.

> In everyday life in Croatia, women lost many of the benefits and rights they had previously achieved; they almost disappeared from public life; violence against women began to grow and women's economic well-being decreased. In independent Croatia's first Parliament, women made up only 5.4 percent of the members. But women had also contested and challenged that situation and searched for different ways of engendering the nation. One of the slogans in the election campaign in Croatia (December 1999) refers to the traditional saying that a woman holds three corners of the house, meaning that woman's power is located in private, at home. Women's groups launched the counter-slogan: *I will exchange one corner of the house for a seat in parliament.*[2]

Under the nationalistic umbrella women lost rights they had already acquired and their feminist knowledge, traditions and subjectivity were endangered. The building of the Nation-State used their symbolic image and their bodies widely, underlining their sexual roles and inscribing them in the topography of the Nation. Family, tradition, the mother-woman, the mother of the soldier, the widow of the national hero, were all glorified. In one of her pieces Rada Iveković states:

> National mythologies draw on traditional gender roles and the nationalist narrative is filled with images of the nation as a mother, wife, and maiden. Practices of nation-building employ social constructions of masculinity and femininity that support a division of labour in which women reproduce the nation physically and symbolically and men protect, defend, and avenge the nation.[3]

Women became a symbolic collective. In the Nation-states that gathered strength throughout the territory of former Yugoslavia, citizenship acquired the flavour of the Nation. Even in the best scenarios, the rights of women derived from the national rights to which they became subordinated.[4]

Citizenship is not a static concept. At different historical times and at different moments, even when referring to the same territory, it is perceived as having different meanings and different practices. In my host country, Italy, I was able to recognise diversified modes through which this concept was applied and codified, according to the origin of the person, their national identity, their gender and the amount of time they had spent on the soil of the host country. I took part in the civil struggles of the excluded, of immigrants who where trying and who still try different ways to have their identities recognised and to obtain acceptance of their 'right to the right to citizenship'. I recognise the emergence of the need for some sort of *mobile citizenship*, separate from nationality, due to the increasing circulation of subjects in intercultural environments, whether refugees, ordinary migrants, 'extracomunitari' (overseas or non–EU citizens), displaced persons... A diversified space with a plurality of identities around us becomes more and more the normal context of our existence. Within this framework, reflective thought on citizenship and on the meanings that the concept implies in contemporary modern and post-modern times includes and emphasises the significance of dignity for each and every one of us.

My personal interest in focusing on the subject 'immigrant woman' within this set of reflections has multiple origins and reflects the importance of promoting human rights as universal and indivisible. But it also recognises the wish to preserve the positioning of feminist subjectivity in what is generally understood as 'universal citizenship' within which immigrant, as well as local, women can easily be subordinated to the hegemony of masculinity. A risk inherent in the idea of universality when addressing citizenship is that the gendered subject remains without recognition and without its own particular history: in effect, without the visibility of women as historical subjects.

2

Criteria for critically observing the concept of citizenship should include taking account of its twofold nature: its normative aspect, as a *status*, i.e. subjects carrying a wide range of rights, and its 'materialisation' as *practice*, involving political participation, broadly defined. Both as a practice and in the relationship between practice and rights, citizenship should be understood as a dynamic process, not as an outcome. Its study is therefore not limited to the analysis of the normative for the same reason that citizenship is much more than just the passive holding of rights; it involves an active engagement with political institutions and the social arena. A similar approach might be useful in overcoming the unilateral concept of citizenship as intrinsically exclusive, drawing boundaries between those who do and do not belong as full members of the national community.[5]

During the 20th century, citizenship was subordinated to nationality, leading, as Gallissot observes[6], to the exacerbation of the opposition between nationals and foreigners, and, from this, to the coalition of nationals *against* foreigners: 'Universalism is only a postulate because it finds itself within *national citizenship* and is therefore reserved only to nationals, can guarantee the *assimilation* for the price of submission and can be put to the service of the *nationalistic project* of the Great Nation'.[7]

In my experience as sociologist-observer, the first outcome (assimilation) takes place predominantly amongst immigrants in the countries of the European Union, whereas the second outcome (the nationalistic project) takes place in a striking way after the dissolution of Yugoslavia into all its successor Nation-States, where the citizens have become prisoners of inter-ethnic relations and of the thrust towards ethnic purification. In both cases, only nationals may be citizens. This is the reason why, from my point of view, the only possible way out of the impasse would be the concept of citizenship understood along the lines of Habermas' definition, namely trying to overcome *national civics* by proposing *another civics,* that which takes place in communication through a relational, political and cultural space, open to intersubjective relationships. In this way, it would be possible to avoid both the crisis and the limitations of national citizenship not only in the sphere of philosophical interpretation but also in everyday practice. Iveković follows the same path when asserting that citizenship is also a co-citizenship, meaning that it can only be exercised from within 'an open political, public, cultural and productive space'.[8] The interaction between one subject and another takes place in this societal dimension of experiencing authentic dialogue and overcoming the traditional subject-object dichotomy.

In this context, I will shift my attention to immigrant women and to the modalities that allow them to become – or hinder them from becoming – social and political actors, while acquiring active citizenship expressed either individually or collectively (or both). It is important not to forget the deep-rooted inequalities that undermine the citizenship rights of those who are considered others, the non-citizens who are positioned on the margins of society.

3

As I have argued elsewhere[9], there are particular conditions imposed by the host society on all migrants before they are allowed, actually and symbolically, to 'enter into the city'. According to the sociologist Adel Jabbar[10], the stages of integration of the foreigner into the host society are as follows:

1. *stabilisation or territorialisation:* first contact with the host society and the search for the necessary means of survival;
2. *urbanisation*, or the stage of *exploration of the territory* and the first institutional contacts that will help the newly arrived to access the networks of services and opportunities;
3. *nativisation*, or the process of social naturalisation derivable from time spent in the territory and from the perception of the symbolic tie between the foreigner and the native citizen;
4. Citizenship *de facto*, or the true *entrance into the city* (right of *civitas*) through daily interrelations, using and participating in public space, which transforms them into effective members of society (political citizenship).

The first phases of the path to integration, *territorialisation, urbanisation* and *nativisation*, are deeply rooted in the sphere of satisfying basic human needs (housing, work, health, formation in the sense of training and qualifications, development of a network of primary contacts within the new physical and social environment) and comprise, therefore, a period of very limited opportunities to become a participative subject, the prerequisite condition for commencing active citizenship and developing a form of human autonomy. In their theorisation of human needs, different authors highlight the link between human autonomy and citizenship. As Ruth Lister inricates, 'Crucial to personal autonomy is the opportunity to participate in social roles of production, reproduction, cultural transmission and political authority. Beyond that lies "critical autonomy – the ability to situate, criticise and, if necessary, challenge the rules and practices" of one's society, in other words, the ability to act as critical citizen'.[11]

Reflecting upon these thoughts in the context of the 'immigrant women's world', persistent questions appear: *What are the real possibilities of obtaining these objectives for women, who are a significant part of the foreign labour-force, if they are absorbed by the economic niches created by a gendered labour market, which leaves only work in domestic service and care, tourism, catering, entertainment, prostitution and sex industries? How, from their disadvantaged economic position and social invisibility, can they acquire the ability to act as (critical) citizens?*

The majority of migrants represent, as Assimina Karavanta states, 'un-constituted subjects', 'subjects without a community', 'un-representable others'. And she adds: 'These others are the body of a different local within the local, a presence and the articulation of a body that challenges the simple binary between local and global by revealing a third incalculable dimension'.[12]

In this relationship between the 'body of a different local within the local', the gap in the occupational levels between autochthonous and immigrant womenis 'inscribed'. Giovanna Campani reminds us of the following general tendency: 'on one hand, there is a movement of European women towards managerial, highly qualified jobs; on the other hand immigrant women are confined to the bottom of the economic scale'.[13] In this process, Campani distinguishes between the position of first generation immigrant women and that of recent migrant women. Nevertheless her conclusion is unambiguous:

> The immigrants are no doubt victims of discrimination and they fill the bottom levels of access to professions. The changes in the

productive structure (...) have contributed to their disadvantaged position in the labour market .[14]

The changes mentioned above are due to economic reorganisation, to the crisis in salaried conditions and to the widening of the grey economy – all conditions where professionalism is underestimated, devalued or denied. Thus, one of the results of such a social and economical environment, typical of female immigration, is *professional disqualification*. This phenomenon causes feelings of frustration and dissatisfaction amongst the population suffering the consequences of disqualification and the loss of identity sources.[15] To overcome this phenomenon will take time, and the situation will only change when there are bilateral or multilateral agreements on the recognition of cross-border qualifications. In the meantime, many professional resources brought by immigrants will be wasted.[16]

Another characteristic of immigrant women who work mostly behind domestic walls and who come back home every day to continue with their family tasks, is *social invisibility*, a common condition for female immigrant populations of different ethnic origins. All these factors make these women vulnerable and their position in relation to active citizenship uncertain.

4

At this point I wish to indicate a new way toward a re-appropriation of citizenship that goes beyond the significance of the normative. This method introduces a *labour of remembrance* through writings and narratives that enable immigrant subjects to forcibly redress forgotten or interrupted experiences. Through cultural productions and writing, immigrant authors rebuild the fragments of their existence, going beyond the private sphere, beyond the boundaries of their history and geography. Word and language become the tools of struggle and the places in which new citizenship takes shape and new states of consciousness are born. The will to share and participate, and the joy in doing so, is demonstrated daily. It seems that in Italian society there is a new dimension on the agenda, that of *being an immigrant.* The idea is slowly and relentlessly entering into the sphere of thought and the 'national' narration through the expressive capacity of migrant writers. Such work announces that we are facing a new epoch in which the 'foreigner' is on the way to becoming perceived as 'mind' rather than only 'hands'. And according to Azade Seyhan, 'the migrant, exile, or voyager not only crosses the threshold into another history and geography but also steps into the role of an itinerant cultural visionary'.[17]

For many women and men, this means *a new birth*, a real 'entry to the city'. In order to make it possible it is necessary to achieve a *favourable global context and internal reconstruction of the host society.* The latter should also be willing to change in the sense defined by Lévinas, as the new candidate-citizens themselves must.

Notes

[1] Vesna Teršelić, 'Expanding our Civil Space: Women in Peace Initiatives' in: Biljana Kašić (ed) *Women and the Politics of Peace*, Centre for Women's Studies, Zagreb 1997, p. 19.

[2] Vesna Kesić, 'Gender and Ethnic Identities in Transition: The Former Yugoslavia – Croatia', in Rada Iveković and Julie Mostov, *From Gender to Nation*, Longo Editore, Ravenna 2002, pp. 63 – 80.

[3] Rada Iveković and Julie Mostov, op. cit. p. 10.

[4] See: Rada Iveković, *Le Sex de la nation*, Non & Non Editions Léo Scheer, France, 2003.

[5] See: Ruth Lister, *Citizenship, Feminist Perspectives*, Palgrave Macmillan, New York, 2003, p. 42.

[6] René Gallissot, 'Cittadinanza', in René Gallissot, Mondher Kilani, Annamaria Rivera, *L'imbroglio etnico*, Edizioni Dedalo, Bari, 2001 pp. 37-64.

[7] René Gallissot, op. cit. p. 62 (Trans. by M.R., italics added).

[8] Rada Iveković, *Le Sex de la Nation*, Non & Non Editions Léo Scheer, France, 2003, p. 24.

[9] See: www. travellingconcepts.net/home.htm

[10] Adel Jabbar, 'Alì dagli occhi azzurri non sa che deve nascere di nuovo' ('Ali with blue eyes does not know that he has to be born again') in 'Dialogica', number 10, Trento, December 1999. pp. 32-44.

[11] Ruth Lister, *Citizenship, Feminist Perspectives*, Palgrave Macmillan, New York, 2003, p. 7.

[12] Assimina Karavanta, *Globalization and the woman-laborer-immigrant: Reconfiguring the 'local', re-thinking the 'global' in women's 'counter-topographies'*, (Athena position paper), p. 65 (see on travellingconcepts.net/home.htm).

[13] Giovanna Campani, *Genere, etnia e classe*, Edizioni ETS, Pisa 2000, p. 128.

[14] Giovanna Campani, op. cit. p. 145.

[15] See: 'Immigrant Women and the Rights of Citizenship', Region Friuli Venezia Giulia, RUE Trieste, October 2002; and Stefania Maggioni, 'Immigrazione al femminile: donne albanesi a Milano', (diploma thesis) Università degli studi di

Milano, academic year 1999/2000.

[16] Melita Richter, 'Donne nel progetto migratorio' (Women in Migratory Project) in AA.VV., *La scala di seta*, Il Ramo d'Oro Editore, Trieste, 2003, p. 36.

[17] Azade Seyhan, *Writing outside the Nation*, Princeton University Press, Princeton and Oxford, 2001, p. 14.

Bibliography

Campani, G. (2000) *Genere, etnia e classe*, Edizioni ETS, Pisa.

Gallissot, R. (2001) 'Cittadinanza', in Gallissot, R., Kilani, M., Rivera, A., *L'imbroglio etnico*, Edizioni Dedalo, Bari.

Immigrant women and the rights of citizenship, Region Friuli Venezia Giulia, (Research) RUE Trieste, October 2002.

Iveković, R. (2003) *Le Sex de la nation*, Non & Non Editions Léo Scheer, France.

_____ (1997) 'Women, Politics, Peace', in Biljana Kašić, ed *Women and the Politics of Peace*, Centre for Women's Studies, Zagreb.

_____ and Mostov, J. eds (2002) *From Gender to Nation*, Longo Editore Ravenna.

Jabbar, A. (1999) 'Alì dagli occhi azzurri non sa che deve nascere di nuovo' ('Ali with blue eyes does not know that he has to be born again') in *Dialogica*, number 10, Trento, December.

Karahasan, Dž. (1998) 'That sentence of the old Rabbi could never be forgotten in Sarajevo', in *Ares*, Roma, no. 1.

Kesić, V. (2002) 'Gender and Ethnic Identities in Transition. The Former

Yugoslavia – Croatia', in Iveković, R. and Mostov, J. eds *From Gender to Nation*, Longo Editore Ravenna, Ravenna.

Lévinas, E. (1992) *Fuori dal soggetto*, (Out of the Subject) Marietti, Genova.

Lister, R. (2003) *Citizenship, Feminist Perspectives* (second edition) Palgrave Macmillan, New York.

Maggioni, S. (1999/2000) *Immigrazione al femminile: donne albanesi a Milan*o, (diploma thesis) Università degli studi di Milano, academic year 1999/2000

Seyhan, A. (2001) *Writing Outside the Nation*, Princeton University Press, Princeton and Oxford.

Richter, M. (2003) 'Donne nel progetto migratorio' (Women in Migratory Project) in AA.VV., *La scala di seta*, Il Ramo d'Oro Editore, Trieste.

Teršelić, V. (1997) 'Expanding our Civil Space: Women in Peace Initiatives' in Biljana Kašić, ed *Women and the Politics of Peace*, Centre for Women's Studies, Zagreb.

Concepts on the road, travelling, embodied and minoritarian: Citizenship, Intersubjectivity and Responsibility

Eva Skærbæk

In comparison with women in other countries, women in Scandinavia are often regarded as having considerably better status. This is a truth that needs some modification. Norway, in which I live and work, has one of the most segregated labour markets in Europe. This means that to a great extent women are doing the traditional caring work, paid (public) and unpaid (private). This influences women's ways of being citizens. In Denmark, research indicates that there is a gendered division between 'little' and 'big' democracy. Thus, in spite of different models in Sweden, Norway and Denmark, the challenge for all of them is to overcome the divide between women's participation in the local politics of everyday life and their lack of inclusion in European and global politics (Siim, 2001).

I was born in March 1945, a few months before the second world war came to an end. In 1960-70 I was busy studying while students protested against the power of men in general and against that of the professors in particular. Later I joked about how I got married while other women revolted. One way of interpreting this is that I was too young and too disciplined, another is that my being at the university was already the result of a protest and a victory. Raised in a home with upper middle class norms and economics, the roles were classic: my father was the provider and my mother the homemaker. The power balance at the university did not surprise me; it was too familiar. And I had won the most important battle, that of leaving home and studying at a university. My life project was very clear to me: I never wanted to be economically dependent on a man. Married or single, I would never go for less than a full-time job. I was so sure that this would lead to equality and a better society. When I had children, one of each sex, I treated them (I thought) equally, thinking that this also would change the power balance and lead to equality. Again, I had overlooked how the sexual contract (Pateman, 1988) maintained the power balance between my husband and me and thereby also infected the children. An everyday situation illuminates this. The children were supposed to clear the table after dinner. One day our three year old daughter began clearing the table, and I interrupted her saying that it could not be her turn again. Her brother, six years old, answered arrogantly: let her do it, she loves it so much. My violent reaction, ordering her to sit down and him immediately to take his turn, told me that there was more at stake here than children's play.

According to Ruth Lister, there are two different images of the ideal citizen. One is the independent citizen of traditional political theory; the other is the citizen who locates herself within the valued bonds of human interdependence.

> It is one of the contradictions of welfare states that, while offering women a degree of economic independence, they, simultaneously,

> tend to construct them as economic dependants, thereby undermining their economic independence (Lister, 2003: 171).

A pivotal constraint, and therefore a target for feminist citizenship praxis, is the domestic division of labour that gives men a collective advantage over women in the public space. '*Time* is a resource for citizenship, generally skewed in favour of men. Citizenship politics is therefore in part about the politics of time' (Lister, 2003: 200). Agreeing with Lister, I find the main problem at stake is that the activity of caring, whether it is public or private, is given only minor recognition. Both the ones in need of care and the ones giving care are defined as dependants in a society that values independent beings over dependent ones. This means low payment and consequently low status, not only for the receivers but also for the givers of care. Care obligations result in men filling the most valued and best-paid jobs in society, while relegating women to low paid, often part-time jobs.

This is much in line with Will Kymlicka's analysis. He argues that equality cannot be achieved by allowing men to build social institutions according to their interests, and then ignoring the gender of the candidates when deciding who fills the roles in these institutions.

> The problem is that the roles may be defined in such a way as to make men more suited to them, even under gender-neutral competition (Kymlicka, 1990: 241).

As consequence women are made dependent on men, which in the case of divorce results in even greater inequality. The more social institutions reflect male interests, the less arbitrary the discrimination. Kymlicka draws the harsh conclusion that male domination over women in society means there is no need to discriminate against them: women will never be in a position to be arbitrarily discriminated against in employment (Kymlicka, 1990).

Kymlicka's analysis is confirmed by a recent research project in the arena of health and social work in Norway. The marginalisation of women in Norway is increasing in many public institutions. While men dominate at the top levels, women are isolated in the middle positions and below. A major problem for most women in this sector is that they are neither seen nor given the recognition they deserve. The work, status and perspectives of women seem to be systematically different from those of men. When women draw attention to the problems they experience, they are labelled as disloyal towards their employers because they render an unwanted picture of the institution. They are conceived as saboteurs.

> The gendered division of labour is fairly common, and the distribution of benefit and influence correlate strongly with this in the way that women hold nearly all the positions where prestige is low and the workload great. The same goes for the evaluation of who has the right and the competence to talk on behalf of the organisation in formal meetings (Likhetens kjønn [The Gender of Equality], 2003: 149).

The problem, as I see it, is that women's dependence and inferior position is not an external layer concealing their essential sameness with men; these conditions are already part and parcel of the construction of femaleness and body image. It extends deep into the structure of the different bodily identity of the female. It influences her way of thinking and working, and it positions her as the sexually different and compliant body in every aspect of sexuality. My point is not new but underlines how important it is to investigate the concept of citizenship from a gendered perspective.

When working to develop an ethical framework through changing the subject/object scheme into one based on intersubjectivity, Beauvoir discovered that this would never work as long as half of the population, women, were not recognised as subjects in their own right, either by themselves, or by the society in which they lived. This drew her to investigate what it is to be a woman (Skærbæk, 2001). Beauvoir never returned to develop an ethics of ambiguity or to the development of intersubjectivity. Instead she became a woman philosopher masquerading as a writer. Rather than reading this as a failure, Linnel Secomb suggests that we see this as an adoption of a minoritarian language and style (1999).

According to Deleuze and Guattari, the function of minor and major language is that the latter is a result of homogeneity and unification while the former allows for variation and diversity. Minoritarian language has been criticised for impoverishing philosophy, but it could also be seen as necessary for making philosophy relevant. Instead of complying with the careful and measured standards of logical reasoning on which philosophy purports to rely, Beauvoir creates a simultaneously impoverished and enriched form, at odds with conventional philosophy.

> By insisting that she is not a philosopher, Beauvoir is able to take liberties with the concepts-creations of her philosophical fraternity and so creates a pastiche plane of thought amenable to variation and transformation (Secomb, 1999: 106).

Creating concepts is not achieved in a vacuum, but from existence in the process of becoming. Utilising Sartre's concept of freedom, Merleau-Ponty's flesh, Hegel's in-itself and for-itself and Heidegger, Mitsein and Husserl's embodied perceptual experience to examine the feminine condition, these concepts change. Absolute freedom becomes limited, the opposition or dialectic of in-itself and for-itself becomes intertwined in the flesh, the antagonistic relationship to the other becomes reciprocity and generosity (Secomb, 1999).

By incorporating philosophical terms within everyday language, Beauvoir may be understood as doing *minoritarian philosophy*. This opens up new dimensions in her thought as well as developing a mode of philosophy useful to feminist philosophers and other marginalised philosophies. Thus inspired to find new ways of thinking and talking, I want to further develop – as Beauvoir did in her time – the connections between the individual woman and the economic, political, social, juridical, educational, familial, medical and governmental situations that shape her. Care, as indicated above, is such a connection.

The basic ontology of human existence is interdependency. Within the framework of interdependency we, men and women, as human beings, are dependent and independent throughout life. This differs radically from the tradition that has taught us to develop from dependency into independent and autonomous adults, a perception which makes a difference in the understanding of care. While traditionally care is recognised as something you can do or not do, in the framework of interdependency care is a necessary condition of life. To live is to care.

In order to be recognised and included as a full citizen in European and global politics it is important to overcome the problem of time constraints. To do that it is important not only to develop but also to integrate an alternative definition and understanding of care. I suggest that we recognise care as the existential condition of life. In this conception care is beyond the constraints of one right way to respond, one right way to live, as there is no age or colour or sex that is the right one (Skærbæk, 2001). This perspective means that every human being from the very beginning of life is inserted as subject, as a citizen with a responsibility to care for other subjects.

To assume responsibility, a human being, adult or child, man or woman, needs to be recognised as a free subject; this recognition, however, needs to be given by another free subject. Everyone needs freedom and recognition, the two key concepts in the Beauvoirian understanding of intersubjectivity:

> To will oneself free is also to will others free, such will is no abstract formula, it points at concrete actions for each one of us (Beauvoir, 1947: s online).

In other words, intersubjectivity is an ethical vision, linked to an understanding of interdependency as the basic ontology of human existence. And this leaves only one real kind of citizen, a citizen who locates her/himself within the valued bonds of human interdependence.

My question is how to make this work/happen. The main focus of my research and teaching is how to understand, teach and practise ethics so that the dignity of the parts involved in the relation and interaction of care is addressed, and if necessary, redressed. I work, teach and conduct research at a University College, Department of Health and Social Studies. Two years ago I was elected as a member of the board of the College. It soon became apparent to me that my department is the least recognised of all departments. Whether this is due to the fact that the majority of the workforce is female, or due to the areas of care and social work which again are linked to women, is not easy to tell. Probably both ingredients work together to reproduce a stigma that is very difficult to change. The leaders of my department realise that they are acting as good girls, following all the rules, and yet they know they can never relax. The staff in this department work more hours than is typical within other departments, and have less time to do research than their colleagues. This dreadful state of affairs is a constant frustration to every one of us.

How do we turn the energy of this frustration into a constructive process of change? Citizenship is an intersubjective enterprise; it cannot be carried out by isolated individuals. To avoid a preoccupation with 'victim feminism', a gendered perspective is necessary in the sense that it allows for a focus on both agency and structural constraints and the interplay between them. What are the necessary strategies, the productive steps, that can be taken towards a recognition of women, the work we do, the knowledge we make, and our contribution as citizens, as subjects, as responsible human beings?

Bibliography

Beauvoir, Simone de (1947) *The Ethics of Ambiguity,* HYPERLINK "http://www.marxists.org/reference/subject/ethics/de-beauvoir/ambiguity/ch02.htm"

Kymlicka, Will (1990) *Contemporary Political Philosophy,* Clarendon Press, Oxford.

Lister, Ruth (2003) *Citizenship: Feminist Perspectives,* New York University Press, New York.

Pateman, Carole (1988) *The Sexual Contract,* Polity Press, Cambridge.

Secomb, Linnel (1999) *Beauvoir's Minoritarian Philosophy,* In Hypatia vol.14, no 4.

Skærbæk, Eva (2001) *Who Cares: Ethical Interaction and Sexual Difference,* Unipub, Oslo.

_____ (2001) *Anerkendelse, frihed, og faglighed* (Recognition, Freedom and Professionalism), Høgskolen i Østfold. Rapport 2005, 2 oplag

Siim, Birte (2001) *Køn, demokrati og modernitet* (Gender, Democracy and Modernity), Hans Reitzel, Copenhagen.

Vike, Halvard (2003) *Likhetens kjøn* (The Gender of Equality), In The Paradoxes of Equality, Universitetsforlaget, Oslo.

Comments on Papers

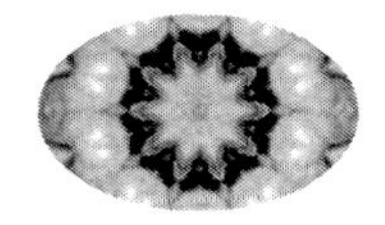

Dasa Duhaček

These texts, while travelling between North and South as well as East and West, have addressed issues of intersubjectivity and citizenship on their own terms, then in relation to each other, and finally by defining them in relation to other concepts such as care, interdependence, reciprocity, nationalism, war, responsibility, among others. In this way, all the texts are rich in inducing reflections as well as in raising many provocative issues.

Some of the texts resonate strongly with a personal investment in theoretical issues, which gives these a specific tone, and sheds light on the genealogies of our theoretical views. In addition, I notice that we have addressed these two pivotal concepts along the following lines: whereas, in regard to citizenship, the papers mostly have a similar point of departure, intersubjectivity has been developed in different directions, sometimes juxtaposed.

Citizenship is approached critically in all the papers; we all register that many of its mechanisms function in ways that exclude some from the privilege of being a citizen. These mechanisms are often brutal and crude: Melita Richter describes this state as the 'absence of rights' while Eva Skærbæk pinpoints *time* as a resource, gendered in its availability. When analysing these processes, Melita is inspired by im/migration, which may prove to be painful even when it is chosen, and is especially so when forced upon people. This stripping away of the 'right to have rights' is the consequence of any war, and Melita relates her argument with great sensitivity to the wars in former Yugoslavia. I find her concept of *mobile citizenship* very valuable as a way of overcoming not only the current constraints, but also the serious threats, and ultimately the deep pitfalls, of nationalism. This concept might have the capacity to override the different borders and boundaries – conceptual and otherwise – of today's nation-states. In effect, the same presupposition comes through in Elena Pulcini's perceptive text, when she writes of the potentials opened up through the processes of globalisation that we often lose sight of, such as the loss of borders and increased openness; her optimism makes a refreshing change in this regard. 'Elsewhere' in relation to any centre is lost and there is a possibility, even if remote, that the same may happen to the 'Other'.

But, importantly, in Melita's text citizenship is a process, and cannot be an end result. And since Elena calls for taking into account the potentials offered by globalisation, and Eva points to the direction and the vehicle of change, they therefore all advocate strongly that we should and can and should set our sights on the future of citizenship in its possible transformations. Elena also rightly draws attention to the fact that these transformations of citizenship, or any other changes for the better, are our own responsibility.

I do, however, find the argument that develops the concept of the Self and reciprocity as opposed to intersubjectivity and care in Elena's paper problematic. The concept of care does need to be divorced from a parental framework, but positioning care in relation to the Other and directing it towards the Other does not, in and of itself, mean equating it with the maternal paradigm. This concept of the Other, as well as the issues of care (for the Other), are more in keeping with the way Lévinas addresses the Other, and he can hardly be understood as representative of a maternal standpoint. I do agree that one point of departure could be care for the Self, but only on the condition that the rationale follows Hannah Arendt's approach. An Arendtian approach would explain that care for the Other – my care for the Other – may be grounded in the Self precisely because I could not live with *myself* otherwise; or, to further draw out the consequences, because I would then have to live with myself as the one who may have consciously chosen to be the source of pain for the Other.

Perhaps part of the problem lies in what I perceive to be Elena's misinterpretation of Arendt's work as 'female', or misconstruing of her idea of 'birth' as having any association with the female and/or women, which is absolutely not the case (Arendt, 1958). Her concept of birth was only a metaphor for 'beginning anew'; it was less inclined to fragility and more towards representing the potential of humanity and the challenge set before each and every one of us; and whereas I do agree that Arendt may see humanity as 'ontologically exposed to otherness', I don't think she argues that this 'dependence' or 'vulnerability' is owing to any 'origin', since this would invoke determinism and essentialism, both of which she was vehemently opposed to. These are precisely the elements of her theory that I find appealing.

Finally, there have always been those who have embraced and deployed care for the Self, turning it only too easily into care for their own selves. The point is precisely not to dwell in shallow, declarative altruism, but in the fact that *care for the Other* has – despite all the declarations – never been implemented in our world; whereas care for the Self has been, and in practice still is, so often recognised and fully operational.

In the insightful reading of Beauvoir as a *minoritarian philosopher* that Eva suggests, we can trace a productive approach to the way we consider and evaluate thinkers. Existentialism here is not of a 'Sartrean' kind, but is infused with care and when addressing our concerns departs from the 'antagonistic relation to the Other' and 'becomes the one of reciprocity and generosity'. Lastly, in Eva's text I found what could become a core theoretical point of departure: placing interdependence as an ontological concept in the place of either independence or dependence; this displaces the false choice between the seductive ideal that is very much present in liberalism – the ideal of independence and its denigrating counterpart, i.e. dependence. Interdependence thus becomes the nodal point of the political.

Elena Pulcini

First of all I would like to thank Eva, Dasa and Melita because, even though we have not had the opportunity to work with each other much in person, I have found our exchanges and discussions very fruitful. To begin with, I feel a profound affinity with Eva when she says that care is not something that is subsidiary or optional, something that can be chosen or disregarded, and it certainly cannot be identified with women's 'natural' tendencies. On the contrary, care is an *ontological* concept that involves us all, men and women, inasmuch as we are all human beings: 'to live is to care', insofar as existence itself is based on interdependency. Thus, I appreciate Eva's ontological perspective, and I generally agree that it is important to theorise – as other feminist thinkers (from Irigaray to Cavarero to Cixous) have proposed, a 'dual ontology' that enhances precisely this relational aspect of existence. But I think that this perspective needs to be integrated with an *anthropological* point of view, reflecting on the subject's roots and very reasons for being. In this connection, I have tried elsewhere to propose the idea of an *anthropology of the neediness* (Pulcini, 2001), going against the Cartesian view of a closed and self-sufficient subject. Instead, I stress 'neediness', a term coined by Martha Nussbaum (2001), of the subject; that is, of a subject *mindful of origin and birth* and therefore aware of its resulting dependency, its insufficiency, which in turn causes it to need care from the other.

This is why I prefer to speak of *reciprocity* rather than *intersubjectivity*; though I believe that the concept of intersubjectivity that Eva formulates, inspired by the reflections of Simone de Beauvoir and closely linked to the idea of 'interdependency', is more fruitful than the Habermasian concept of intersubjectivity, which tends to overshadow the concrete and experiential side of the subject, ridding it of its singularity and uniqueness. In this sense, I think that if Eva were to pay greater attention to the concept of 'recognition', her analysis would be further enhanced. Indeed, the theme of recognition, which has become a topic of fervent reflection, stresses the fact that, in order to be able to speak of equality and equal dignity, it is not enough to produce the material conditions to allow for access to equal opportunities in terms of justice and equity in managing resources, but it is also necessary to give every person, every person's *identity*, equal dignity and worth.

I think that consideration of the concept of recognition could also bear fruit for Melita, who deals with the problem of immigrant women and proposes a complex concept of citizenship as a practice, which also implies political participation. The position of immigrant women suffers not only from a reduction in rights, but also from more or less explicit forms of 'disregarding' their identity. Everything concerning their history, their traditions, their 'differences' is either denied or strongly neglected by an idea of citizenship that is confirmed as being essentially exclusive and founded on nationalistic premises. This means also rethinking the very idea of 'rights', which in my opinion could be formulated more effectively through the idea of '*capability*' proposed by Amartya Sen and Martha Nussbaum (Amartya Sen, *Inequality Reexamined*, Oxford University Press 1992; Martha C. Nussbaum, *Women and Human Development: The Capabilities Approach*, Cambridge University Press, Cambridge and New York, 2000). This concept arises from the observation that we can often have rights, that is, be legally entitled to particular rights, without possessing the capability to actively exercise them. This 'capability' alludes not only to what we are legally recognised to have and are objectively given, but also to what we are *actually* able to do, in purely subjective terms, in order to achieve authentic dignity and autonomy.

I also agree with Dasa about the importance of the concept of responsibility; however, I try to base this on the idea of reciprocity. Dasa is right when she argues, following Lévinas, that responsibility must not be seen as 'a comfortable expectation of reciprocity'. Indeed, it is in this sense that I propose 'reciprocity' as being what is triggered by the feeling that we are always simultaneously the *subject and object* of responsibility, or rather, as I try to claim in my paper, of *care*. In other words, reciprocity consists of the fact that only a subject who acknowledges that he needs care is capable of caring for the other.

Dasa's paper has also allowed us to reflect on what I would like to define as the obscure and threatening sides of the figure of the other. While quoting Butler, Dasa wonders: 'what happens when the other uses violence against me, when he actually acts as an enemy', an aggressor? The problem is real and cannot be avoided, as it produces the awareness that the *ethical* meaning of the idea of the other is not simply and immediately intrinsic to the figure of the other. It requires a series of mediations that allow us to find strategies so that the other, the enemy, becomes the interlocutor to be taken into account, the one whom we make the object of our care and responsibility.

Finally, there is the problem of the relationship between responsibility and power. Dasa says that Beauvoir maintains there is a close relationship between these two concepts and that responsibility must be attributed in proportion to the position of power held. Dasa seems to agree with this, but then she alludes to the women's movement in Serbia as a form of taking responsibility, starting from the bottom, in a context that does not constitute institutional power, but, on the contrary, resists it. I would like Dasa to clarify this point, because I do not fully agree with this mobilisation of the close relationship between responsibility and power; or rather, I am convinced that today, above all in the face of global challenges, those in power must claim responsibilities that were not so necessary before (e.g. towards the environment and future generations), but I am also convinced that today responsibility must and can be taken in an essentially subjective (and not just institutional) manner. In a world that is 'out of control', overrun with new challenges and epoch-making threats, we are all called upon to take responsibility towards the other, meaning not only our neighbour, but the planet, humanity, the biosphere: a responsibility that, as women well know after eons of experience, begins with our small everyday actions, with many small deeds, which can add up to resistance against the destructive processes that we are witnessing today.

Melita Richter

I find Elena's view of globalisation useful as a general framework within which to place and discuss the concepts of care, recognition and reciprocity in the Habermasian senses of the terms. At the same time I have the feeling that the radically new nature of the process of globalisation on which Elena focuses, and which would be the creation of a 'single world in which there are potentially no barriers between *us* and *them* any more', is somehow deprived of its inner complexity (inequalities, separations, hierarchies of power relations, gender asymmetries...). At the end of her paper Elena underlines the universality of the ontological essence of humanity and the world in which 'we all are exposed to the same risks and called upon to respond to the same challenges, caught up as we are by a common destiny'. This approach reflects a perfect circulation of philosophical thought, but IF we try to ground it in our experiential field, I would strongly doubt the existence of such a single world with (potentially) 'no barriers between *us* and *them* any more'. If we just cast a glance at our neighbour, the Balkans, we can see how new barriers and frontiers are arising and dividing European soil and identity into fragmented units based on the concepts of inclusion/exclusion rather than on European integration and unity. This process of fragmentation creates in the same part of the continent a profound gap in its geographical and mental maps, in culture and in the ability to de-codify its present, through the false separation of its memories and its aspirations.

The Balkan example is only one, close to home, that introduces the category of *historical time*, underlining contradictions in the aspirations of fragmented parts of Europe to create Nation States (often led by absurd ideologies of 'ethnically pure territories'), while at the same time, the other European states are investing considerable effort to create a single supranational political, economic and juridical entity. Without even turning our attention to 'third world' countries, can we really we say that the destiny of these European societies is the same? And could their citizens perceive them as such? Are we not exposed to the creation of new administrative borders with stronger impediments to free movements of people in these specific areas (new visa systems, new pauperisation of the population, new social erosion, old/new exclusion along ethnic, race, religious, or ideological lines)? And can we so easily dismiss from our minds the increasing walls around us, not only the symbolic protection of Fortress Europe, but also the ones between Israeli Jewish and Palestinian populations? Or the wall around Ceuta and Melilla, 'parts of Europe in Africa'? Can we forget the images of the recent assault on the huge wire wall in these localities by desperate African subjects and the violent reaction of the border police exercising the protection of 'mirage Europe?' And the growing wall between the USA and Mexico? Or the ethnic wall between Albanian and Serb populations in Kosovo? And the similar one between Greek and Turkish populations in Cyprus? And the old/ new separation inside the internal body of some Western countries, such as France with its burning suburbs and the creation of ever more evident inner tensions between centres and peripheries.

Not only are new fears increasingly haunting the inhabitants of the external area of the European Union, but they are also materialising as mental maps in human relations among citizens and the institutions that once more tend to apply the principle of exclusion as a basic principle of society's security. The border, once an external line and container of the safety of the state, has moved towards the interior, broken and diffused in the internal space, where it is cavorting in front of and around some (in)visible adversary. Is this not also a debt owed to globalisation?

'Potentially', says Elena, the 'other' is no more. But, she continues: 'the *other* lives in our neighbourhood, mixed into the chaos of our metropolises, passes beyond confines, across territories, in frenzied and ungovernable migration'. So, the Other still exists and represents a threat to the *we* group. But it is *another* 'Other.' What would be the difference between these two 'Others'? Can we translate (always and again) the new Otherness from a gender perspective, alluding to Simone de Beauvoir's thesis, as other participants in this discussion have suggested? The answer is no doubt extremely complex, but it would give us a clearer view of the dynamics of change within the inner soul of our 'potentially' single world. In this potentiality lies our future.

I am aware that all my considerations stimulated by Elena's contribution are of a socio-political character, while her text is a philosophical one. This fact might lead us to believe that the two approaches cannot come together and must preserve their disciplinary distance. In the last instance, I think that the meeting ground of the two might be experiential, the *reality* that affects human lives in specific geopolitical areas of the world.

Here comes my only methodological interrogation of Elena's paper: it deals with universal philosophical categories; it never touches the ground and, somehow, manages to evade one of our original guiding questions:

> *'What is/could be the impact of these concepts in different cultural, geopolitical and professional contexts and daily life practices?'*

What I do consider to be Elena's contribution to our debate is her development of the concepts of responsibility, recognition and the notion of the contaminated subject. I continue to find the relation/confrontation between the contributions of Elena and Dasa extraordinarily challenging.

Dasa defines herself as a political theorist with a background in philosophy. Her text reflects her philosophical background but, unlike Elena's, it is well grounded in a specific geopolitical and cultural context: Serbia, the Western Balkans. Theoretical analysis has a personal meaning for her. Dealing with the question of the relationship between *citizenship* and *responsibility*, she positions her philosophical approach in her own society. She specifies a *concrete civil society* and its role in the opposition to Milosevic's regime (here the responsibility of the government is no longer a philosophical concept but a real challenge). And she focuses on this from a gender perspective (the role of women in the opposition movement and peace activism). In this context she has no difficulty in speaking in the first person, which allows her to express her personal feelings of mourning, of anger, of renunciation… and which enables her to recognize HER 'whole world for what it was – as it was falling apart'.

I probably feel closer to Dasa's approach because it engages the world of which I am also a part. When Dasa uses the descriptive verb 'falling apart' we both know that it conceals other meanings – those of war, of war crimes, of new separations and exclusions of Otherness, of the loss of plural identity…. One step forward might be to think through both Dasa and Elena's conceptualisations of responsibility: in Dasa's case as 'political responsibility for our political choices' and the importance of asking 'what is MY responsibility for the Other?'; in Elena's, taking responsibility for global processes ('radicalisation of evil', 'nuclear threat', the 'possibility of losing the world').

Reflecting more deeply on this difference I see each approach as related to different ethical spheres and different modes of acting within public/private space. While in Dasa's interpretation, responsibility involves facing the past and looking towards the future in Lévinas's sense of *responsibility to/for the Other*, Elena's understanding of the concept is tightly linked to the idea of a common human destiny, in which we are all affected by the same events and share (following Hans Jonas) the worry about the possibility of losing the world that hosts humanity. For that reason and from this deep *fear of loss*, we as individuals must ourselves take on responsibility. Responsibility thus finds its sources in awareness that the world needs caring for, but a kind of caring inextricably bound to *care for the Self*.

But how would it be possible to think about responsibility for the current global situation(s), without trying to see its links to the asymmetrical structure of power relations and of decision-making on a global, but also on a specific local, geopolitical level? Would it involve developing different public reasoning and different praxis? And how different really is the question of responsibility for the government to which citizens give their express or tacit consent (Dasa's demand and her firm answer: citizens are the ones who should bear that responsibility) from Elena's insistence that we recognise the hierarchical dissonance between the Self and the Other? These reflections can only be the beginning of a larger conversation about intersubjectivity, citizenship and responsibility, which would need much more space to include all of our thoughts and differences.

Eva's paper made me aware of a surprising number of similarities between the South and the North of the continent, between women's positioning (or new marginalisation?) in a Mediterranean and a Scandinavian country. Similarities in inequality could be compared to confirm the reproduction of the asymmetrical power balance and asymmetrical gender recognition in both societies. Eva brings the feeling of *frustration* into our analysis and questions whether and how we might turn the energy of this frustration into a constructive process of change.

The need for change is strongly present in all our contributions. Eva also raises the question of a necessary strategy in the production of steps towards recognition of women. Dasa draws on the example of women peace activists undertaking restructuring and re-conceptualising citizenship as responsibility to the Other in their political community. My focus on the transformation of 'non-citizens' into 'citizen subjects of policy' primarily concerns immigrant women who cross the threshold of the host society burdened with the consciousness that the latter should also be willing to change (Lévinas).

And last but not least, Eva also offers an example of an everyday situation from her family narrative. Her story underlines the extent to which we need to struggle for justice and further affirms the need for an ethics of justice in our everyday lives. At the same time, Eva reminds us how important our biographical history is for sustained, politicised thinking.

Eva Skærbæk

The reflections of Elena, Melita and Dasa have, each in their own way, extended and challenged my world and my way of thinking and living.

With Elena I share the desire to free the phenomenon of care from the maternal dimension. Care has been and still is intertwined with oppressive gender divisions. As Bubeck puts it: 'Care is done by women, it is associated with women and it expresses and symbolises femininity' (Bubeck, 1998: 26). My research has convinced me that it makes a difference whether care is considered an inherent part of the interdependency of all human beings as human beings or whether it is limited to parental/maternal care or to a common social practice, as Selma Sevenhuisen suggests would be useful (Sevenhuijsen, 1998). Only when care is considered an existential condition of life will it be possible to see it as something beyond the constraints of one right way to respond, one right way to live. This understanding, together with my work in the field of care and social work, makes me somewhat reluctant to accept some of the words Elena uses when developing her theory. Needs and contamination already carry negative connotations when they refer to bodies, the bodies of women. The same goes for vulnerability and fragility, although they are slightly less negative. Language is power and vice versa, and I am anxious that Elena's vocabulary, instead of freeing care from its maternal dimension, may reinforce the connection. Instead of an 'anthropology of neediness', as proposed by Elena, I therefore suggest an ontology of interdependency.

In my view every human being is a subject in itself from its very beginning, both dependent and independent throughout life. Thus my understanding of interdependency relates to intersubjectivity as a means of obtaining real citizenship. Consequently, I am critical of Elena's suggestion that we exchange the concept of intersubjectivity for that of reciprocity. Elena argues that intersubjectivity, at least in the Habermasian definition, risks reducing subjectivity to a socio-linguistic construction, neglecting the concrete dimensions lived by subjects. My understanding of subject and intersubjectivity, however, is inspired by Simone de Beauvoir, and by Jessica Benjamin and Elisabeth Grosz, who each in their own way have developed Beauvoir's understanding of the ambiguous subject. In combining a philosophy of history with a phenomenological description of individual experience, Beauvoir presents an ethical approach that rests on the complex interaction and reciprocal implication of the spheres of subjectivity and sociality. By emphasising the ambiguous condition of life this approach points to ways of understanding how inequality is produced and how at the same time it suggests change, not only as a possibility but also as a responsibility.

The crucial point in this theory of intersubjectivity is that the self meets – and is met by – another self in its own right. The recognition that the child has needs is something that the mother is able to give, Benjamin maintains, only by virtue of her own independent subjectivity (Benjamin, 1988). Instead of a meeting between a subject and an object, a subject meets another subject. This subject is embodied, and embodied differently as to sex. Insistently, Grosz argues that the body is the centre, the 'stuff' of subjectivity. By envisioning sexual difference and sexuality together with embodiment, Grosz's theory has given us useful tools to interpret how the female body and female subjectivity are conceived as different from men's bodies and identities. As Hegel, Kant and Habermas understand intersubjectivity, all knowledge is subjective, but there are situations common to more than just one person. The more independently such agreement arises, the more 'truth' there is in such agreement. In this definition, intersubjectivity in terms of agreement between persons replaces the concept of truth. This is a tempting definition, but the core issue of intersubjectivity, as I understand it, is the opposite. Here the vision is to be able to disagree while still recognising the Other. On a Danish poster there is a picture of a worker stating: 'Agreement is not necessary for working together, respect is'.

This makes my position, in this context, more in line with Dasa's. Facing the past with responsibility, Dasa – inspired by Lévinas – suggests, means that we build the future through responsibility to/for the Other. This is not a symmetrical but an asymmetrical relation. The *face* of the Other demands that I respond without demanding – or expecting – reciprocity. One of the ways to connect political practice with care for the Other is through the concept of intersubjectivity, as in practice it presupposes that the one demanding and the one responding recognise each other as subjects. Thus the concept of intersubjectivity may create a bridge between ethics and politics. Reading Arendt, Dasa did find a way to 'critically look upon and recognise my world for what it was – as it was falling apart', and I cannot but admire how Dasa uses this insight to link responsibility for what her government has done in her name together with responsibility for the Other as the essential, primary and fundamental structure of subjectivity.

Reading Melita and her substantial arguments for suggesting citizenship as a mobile and not a static concept, it suddenly occurred to me how important that also is. By moving from Denmark to Norway I lost my right to vote, in either country. Although it would be an insult to immigrant women to suggest that I am in the same situation as they are, we do have something in common. We want to be more than simply passive holders of rights, we want to actively engage in political institutions and in the wider social sphere. It does not suffice to have power at and within the home, as Melita underlines by quoting the wonderful counter-slogan in the election campaign in Croatia 1999: 'I will exchange one corner of the house for a seat in parliament'. In other words, a dichotomy still in need of transgression is the traditional divide between public and private. Not only immigrant women, but in fact a lot of women struggle with how to act as critical citizens from a disadvantaged economic position and from a 'position' of social invisibility. To me this makes it even more important to work together, practising nomadic subjectivity and thereby supporting each other. In short, then, for me, citizenship is a co-citizenship, in the sense that it requires intersubjectivity.

Additional References for Eva's work

Benjamin, Jessica (1988) *The Bonds of Love: Psychoanalysis, Feminism, and the Problem of Domination,* Pantheon, New York.

Bubeck, Diemut (1995) *Care, Gender, Justice,* Clarendon Press, Oxford.

Grosz, Elizabeth (1995) *Space, Time and Perversion. Essays on the Politics of Bodies,* Routledge, New York and Allen and Unwin Sydney.

_____ (1994) *Volatile Bodies. Toward a Corporeal Feminism,* Indiana University Press, Bloomington and Allen and Unwin, Sydney.

Sevenhuijsen, Selma (1998) *Citizenship and the Ethics of Care,* London, Routledge.

Responses to Comments

Dasa Duhaček

The intellectual exchange between Elena, Eva, Melita and myself is becoming an exciting space for me, where the ideas around which my work revolves are tested and sifted, so as to crystallise into theoretically productive concepts and politically useful arguments. And for this I am grateful to them all.

However, there may have been some misunderstandings in our exchange. For example, Elena has read in my text that while quoting Butler I ask the question: 'what happens when the other uses violence against me, when he actually acts as enemy…?' This misreading may point to some of the sources of our differences; since in fact there is no such question in my text. I do quote Butler regarding her interpretation of Lévinas' concept of the Other, but the problem for Butler (and for myself) is quite different from how it is represented: 'What if there is an Other who uses violence against another Other?' *This* is the problem concerning the Other that I am very much concerned with; it is about how different Others relate to each other and the consequences this may have for my political engagement. This is the problem that Butler raises, and in fact she does not look into 'the obscure and the threatening sides to the figure of the other' that Elena mentions.

Elena also asks that I clarify the position of women and/or feminist peace activists in my region (Western Balkans) in the context of power relations. My point was that their activities were certainly not a part of existing power relations, but were and could instead only be an intervention into, and therefore a subversion of, these. As such these activities were only *aiming* at reconceptualising power, and were an attempt at reconstructing citizenship as responsibility to the Other.

The category of reciprocity appears to have raised the most controversy in our texts. Elena still maintains its significant position in that 'reciprocity consists of the fact that only a subject who acknowledges that he needs care is capable of caring for the other…' This is, of course, quite the opposite of what Lévinas would claim, but the fact that Lévinas opposes it may not in and of itself be a crucial critical argument for dismissing this standpoint. A more important and straightforward challenge would be that reciprocity as explained above uses Self as a point of departure, and therefore care for the Self is a primary concern spilling over into a political priority; it is thus inconsistent with care for the Other and consequently does not entail citizenship as a responsibility to (and even less for) the Other. This is why I believe that Eva's point that the face of the Other demanding response without reciprocity is intersubjectvity in practice may be more in keeping with what I would like to argue for. Melita's well-documented and detailed list of exclusions, borders, walls, fears and her passionate outcry for recognising all of these in their concrete appearance resonates with a knowledge of the world and an engagement of a deeply concerned theorist for our/her world.

I would like to add that disciplinary boundaries do not apply when assessing the critical issues of our times. Moreover, many key figures of *contemporary* philosophy not only acknowledge that but also cannot emphasise enough their concern for what Melita has named socio-political issues, since they consider their responsibility to the other/Other their primary task (Bernstein, 2000).

Elena Pulcini

I would like to begin with Melita's comments, in order to clarify an essential point and prevent any misunderstandings. If it is true that globalisation is an ambivalent process, which simultaneously produces homologation and fragmentation, my problem is whether we can come out of this two-pronged situation through our realisation that we are a *common humanity* hosted in a single world. This does not mean denying differences, quite the contrary, we need to fight against both homologation and fragmentation at the same time, so much so that elsewhere I have proposed the idea of a *cosmopolis of differenc*es (Pulcini, 2001), which also means thinking through the concept of *citizenship* from a global perspective.

This does not derive from an optimistic vision of reality, as Dasa seems to imply. Indeed, alas, I am deeply pessimistic. And I wonder if *in the present day* we possess a subjectivity that is able to face up to global challenges. All this is not, to respond to Eva, in contrast to an ontology of interdependence, which I propose to integrate with an anthropological perspective. This is what gives rise to my proposal for a *contaminated subject*, which implies an *anthropology of neediness, of vulnerability.* Only a subject aware of its own fragility, finiteness and dependence is capable of taking its own responsibility and transforming it into care for the other. It is this subject that provides the basis for my concept of *reciprocity*, which I continue to prefer to that of *intersubjectivity*.

This subject, again to respond to Dasa, has nothing to do with the modern and monological Cartesian Self. On the contrary, in the world without confines produced by globalisation, it is indeed an open subject, exposed to the other, or to use Lévinas' words, to the other's 'call'. However, Lévinas does not convince me with his emphasis on the idea of the other as what comes 'before' the Self. I think that we must overcome the dichotomy between selfishness (the Self comes before the other) and altruism (the other comes before the Self) in order to enhance the idea of 'being-with' (Nancy, 1996).

Secondly, and again with the aim of overcoming that opposition, I propose freeing the concept of care from the maternal paradigm. Eva seems to agree with this, while Dasa criticises it. My objective is to free the concept of care from an *altruistic* meaning, also assumed in the Lévinasian perspective proposed by Dasa, to instead make it the ethical expression of a *contaminated subject*, that is, a subject that is himself aware of his own need for care.

Finally, I would like to respond to a fundamental objection levelled against my work by all three of my interlocutors concerning the fact that in my paper there are no personal or biographical references. Maybe the main reason is that my debt towards female thought is so profound and so indissolubly mixed with other moments of my life and my research that at times I do not feel the need to express it, thinking that it appears clear from my very choice of concepts and theoretical perspectives. In other words, without female thought I could never have formulated the idea of the contaminated subject, reciprocity, and care as elements that are for me essential for an anthropology of modernity and the global age.

Additional Reference for Elena's Work

Nancy, Jean-Luc (1996) *Être-avec* in Jean-Luc Nancy *Etre singulier pluriel*, Galilée, Paris.

Melita Richter

It seems that the most demanding and interesting part of our work is just beginning as we are about to conclude our writings.

It seems that we are all agreed on certain ways of illuminating our concepts, i.e. seeing citizenship as a process, not reducing it to the passive possession of rights, but developing it through participation and active commitment in political decisions, and individualising the need for a kind of *mobile citizenship* to overcome its reductive implementation. On the other hand, we have begun a fruitful debate about different interpretations of the concepts of 'responsibility', 'reciprocity', 'intersubjectivity' and 'care' (and others were inevitably introduced into the debate: 'capability', 'rights', 'politics'...). These were read through different theoretical lenses and positioned in the field of diverse individual and collective experience. Our discussion could continue; it has widened our horizons, not closed or cast a shadow over them.

Thanks to all for your comments, suggestions and criticism, which have broadened the scope of my own approach and helped us to create the relational ground needed for inter/transcultural dialogue.

I appreciate Elena's suggestion of bringing in the concepts of *recognition* and capability when discussing the position and rights of immigrant women, to link recognition to *the capability to act in the public sphere and to rethink the very idea of rights*. This is precisely what I meant when I spoke about the *participative subject* as a precondition for the development of *active citizenship* and the ability to *act as a critical citizen*. And it is also important not to lose the correlation between this acknowledgement and the autochthonous female population, which has experienced the emancipation process but still finds itself in a marginal and subordinate position and without real recognition of its dignity. Elena has also reminded us that 'it is not enough to produce the material conditions to allow for access to equal opportunities in terms of justice and equity in managing resources, but it is necessary to give every person, every person's *identity*, equal dignity and worth.' This is essential for our debate. I need search no further for the philosophical support to underline that here we are again speaking about recognition, a *symmetrical recognition* of subjects. It brings to mind the saying of an old Rabbi somewhere in Central Europe, long ago: '*I am I, because you are you – you are you, because I am I.*'[1] This sentence helps us to understand that in order to recognise, articulate and be aware of our own identity, we must first recognise the other, recognise what we have in common with others and therefore what marks our belonging to something (language identity, state identity, other forms of cultural identities), and then – and only then – what marks us out of the collective and makes us unique. This entails recognition of the subjective 'You/I' and the relation between them. And we should not forget that the subject is always *a relation*, a process, a creation; it is the principal agent of change.

Can we say this when we have in mind the creation of the *female subject*? No doubt our minds will be beset by notions such as *non-subject, pseudo-subject, feminist subject,* all parts of our common heritage. But I think that we need to move farther from the subjective and raise the problem of *women as a political group* (and I do not mean this in an institutional sense!). As Rada Iveković notes, this question of women as a political group 'has always been thwarted with all universal, particular and individual means and has not been supported by history. It is up to us to build such relations that history will support us'.[2] The demand Iveković is making is not that '*we also* enrol in history' but that we question *how* we enrol in it, in light of the fact that agreeing on a right way means 'that we are also writing that history. To become its subjects'.[3]

It is exactly this that the women's movement in Serbia, and in all areas of former Yugoslavia where such a movement developed, tried to do. And here I am adding my thoughts to those Elena is formulating regarding the relationship between *responsibility* and *power*, referring to Dasa's example of the women's movement in Serbia as a form of 'taking responsibility, starting from the bottom, in a context that does not constitute power, but, on the contrary, resists it'. My comment at this point would be that the resistance of the women of former Yugoslavia to the nationalist discourse exceeds the narrow relation of *responsibility-power* and inscribes itself in women's refusal to be evacuated from the historical scenario of their own society, or to be erased as historical subjects.

To conclude, I would like to add my very brief reflection to the much discussed concept of *care*. As was confirmed in all our approaches, care has always been considered a minority field and was/is traditionally considered the domain of women's work. This work is not given the recognition it deserves. Eva offers us abundant examples of what it means in a concrete workplace where the majority of that workforce is female and while the area of care and social work is intrinsically linked to women. But she also gives a very articulate definition of *care as the existential condition of life*. This would indicate that care transcends the gendered division of working spheres and embraces the universal, infusing it with unique ethical value. I myself find the concept of care the constituent part of a typically masculine domain, the one of politics. And I wonder: would it not be politics (in a Platonic sense) where care for the Self, for the Other, for potential humanity, for the entire world, is pivotal? If the answer is affirmative, then at least in theory, we should be able to free care of its historical stigma and to reposition it among the most noble universal dimensions of life.

Notes

[1] See in Dževad Karahasan, 'That sentence of the old Rabbi could never be forgotten in Sarajevo', in Ares, Roma, no. 1, 1998, p. 69.

[2] Rada Iveković, *Women, Politics, Peace*, in Women and the Politics of Peace, Centre for Women's Studies, Zagreb, 1997, p.104.

[3] Rada Iveković, op. cit. p.104.

Eva Skærbæk

As a young academic in my first job in the 1970s I sometimes daydreamed of only being a housewife. I had a full-time job, a husband and two children. Brought up as a member of the upper middle class I decided, as mentioned above, that I would never be dependent on a man the way my mother was. The problem was that I, together with most of my generation, had been 'double programmed', as I heard it termed a few years ago, at a seminar in Sweden. According to my identity construction I *had to* meet every expectation in order to feel satisfied. Not only did I/women have to do so much more than our fathers in order to have our work recognised, I/we also had to do about as much as our mothers in order to meet expectations at home. This was more or less the precondition of being allowed to work. Very few of us succeeded in escaping this double programme, and it still seems to prevail. The sixties and seventies were roaring in many respects but not when it came to challenging this predicament. I think this is because so many of us forgot to look critically into our own lives. As Sandra Bartky says:

> We need to understand better than we do now, not only the processes of personality development, but the 'micropolitics' of our most ordinary interactions, the ways in which we inscribe and re-inscribe our subjection in the fabric of the ordinary. The most prominent features and many of the subjective effects of this inscription can be grasped independently of any particular theory of personality formation. We need to locate our subordination not only in the hidden

> recesses of the psyche but in the duties we are happy to perform and in what we thought were the innocent pleasures of everyday life (Bartky, 1990: 119).

This is about intersubjectivity and citizenship, and it is about recognition. It is so basic and yet so difficult. In 2001 I argued that 'a presupppostition of ethical interaction in the public sphere as well as in the private sphere is to recognise equally the different embodiment of the "other" sex, how she lives, works, thinks, loves, relates and generates knowledge. Such recognition will produce a redefinition of subjectivity compelling both sexes to value and position equally the difference of other "others", irrespective of sex, race, sexual preferences, age, class' (Skærbæk, 2001: 4). Since then I have become even more intrigued by the concept of recognition. In my recent research I found the link between recognition, freedom and professionalism to be so important that it became the title of my book (Skærbæk, 2003; see also Skærbæk, 2004).

So to Elena's suggestion that I should pay more attention to recognition, I can only agree, admitting that there is still a lot to say and especially to do in respect to this concept. It is so easy to say that each human being has a unique value that must be recognised, and so difficult to integrate this insight into the concrete life of societies, institutions and teaching as well as our private lives. I think this is linked to whether we understand the human being as an interdependent or as an autonomous being. If recognition is linked to autonomy and thus to the old subject/object system, it fixes rather than liberates the other. If it is linked to an understanding of interdependency, it acknowledges and allows for, maybe even expects, changes.

For the fairly senior students (last year the average age was 44 years) whom I teach and coach, this one year of further education at University College means the beginning of a major change in both their professional and their private lives. The most difficult task for the students – and their teachers – is to link the theory they learn to the practice they perform. What I want to underline is that it takes some courage to break out of the recognition that wants to fix you in your old patterns, the way you were and still are. Maybe it is time to take on the understanding that we are indeed models and therefore have to observe critically how concepts are situated, not only in our professional but also in our personal daily lives. Again, a personal daily life experience might illustrate this: while still young and divorced I told my son one evening that I was leaving to attend a jazz concert. He responded with surprise: but you never do this. And I said: no, but I am doing it now.

Discussing, wondering and pondering over citizenship and intersubjectivity and all the additional concepts with Elena, Dasa and Melita has stirred, enlarged, and moved my understanding, my knowledge, and myself in regards to the key concepts and thus to what we should be most concerned about. The discussion has made me even more conscious of how important it is to be concrete and personal when translating key feminist concepts to colleagues and into education. And of how necessary it is to continue the discussion, especially since it demonstrates how far we can get in developing 'new' knowledge when our own, although different, knowledge is recognised and challenged by colleagues. Such dialogues are what prevent war and violence, so let's keep up the good work and continue that challenge and recognition.

Additional References for Eva's Work

Bartky, Sandra (1990) *Femininity and Domination,* Routledge, New York.

Skærbæk, Eva (2003) *Anerkendelse, frihed, og faglighed* (Recognition, freedom and professionalism), Høgskolen i Østfold. Rapport 2005, 2 oplag.

_____ (2004) It takes two to tango-on knowledge prodution and intersubjectivity *Nora: Nordic Journal of Women's Studies,*Vol 12: 2.

A note from Ann Kaloski of Raw Nerve Books

email: post@rawnervebooks.co.uk web: www.rawnervebooks.co.uk

Dear Reader,

You have in your hands a book from Raw Nerve, a not-for-profit, micro publishing company that draws together people who work 'for love and politics' in order to further thinking about women's lives and feminism.

There was a lot of love and a lot of politics in this project! Travelling Concepts involved about thirty women and a few men living in many different countries – people who wrote, co-ordinated, edited, proofed, designed, organised printing and maintained the accounts. Working with varying styles of thinking and practices as well as sentence construction and referencing systems was an invigorating process from which, I think, we all benefited, and Raw Nerve has tried to retain the diversity of each group's product while bringing the books together into a harmonious series.

I'd like to express my gratitude to the adventurous Travelling Concepts women who wrote the four books – Silvia, Liana, Therese, Mina, Veronica, Dasa, Joan, Melita, Giovanna, Ulla, Enikő, Josefina, Päivi, Luz, Biljana, Soula, Iris, Eva, Sabine, Elena, Sara and not least Clare who facilitated the group so inspiringly and who was a hard-working co-editor. Thanks are also due to Liz, Lee and Karen; Dave and everyone at York Publishing Services; Bob; Ulla (again) and Josephine; the Centre for Women's Studies and Athena 2; and especially to our designer Hilary who has accommodated, interpreted and balanced the visions of a large group of sassy women with patience and care.

If you enjoyed this publication, consider buying one of the other books in the series (see the full list in the Series Preface). You are also invited to join in the wiki-based discussion at www.travellingconcepts.net

Ann